"Donna Gaines has captured the cry of o
intimacy with God. Vividly she paints th
tionship with Him—and the strength and power God gives for us
to continue on that journey. She skillfully identifies the obstacles
to discovering the 'more' that God has for us and clearly shows the
provision God has made through His Word and the indwelling
Holy Spirit to help each of us experience the abundance He has
planned for us. Written for women, *There's Gotta Be More* clearly
has a message for us all."

Jimmy and Carol Ann Draper
President Emeritus, LifeWay Christian Resources

"Are you a wishbone Christian, always wishing for more victory,
more power, more fruit of the Spirit? This is a book for wishbone
Christians. Donna Gaines in *There's Gotta Be More* sets forth with
clarity and conviction the ways to discover the 'more' that God offers
to every believer. This book touches virtually every aspect of fullness
of life in Christ. One cannot read it with an open mind and spiritual
hunger without coming away from the book infinitely richer."

Roy J. Fish, ThD
Distinguished Professor of Evangelism Emeritus,
Southwestern Baptist Theological Seminary

"The subtitle of this book is *Enjoying the Spirit-Filled Life,* and that
is exactly what Donna Gaines encourages us to do in this work. It
is bursting with fresh illustrations, skillful application, and excel-
lent biblical insights. Her challenge to all believers is to eagerly
seek Christ with all our hearts—and experience the true joy that
will follow. You will be a better Christian for having read *There's
Gotta Be More.*"

Susie Hawkins
Bible Study Teacher, Women's Ministries Consultant

"I personally love to read a book that describes life's experiences.
As you read *There's Gotta Be More,* you will see a story unfold of a
hunger that settles for nothing less than God's best, the Spirit-filled
life. Read it and be blessed!"

Johnny Hunt
Senior Pastor, First Baptist Church, Woodstock, Georgia

"Donna Gaines has masterfully penned a volume for every woman who has ever longed for a more intimate relationship with her Lord. Let yourself be encouraged by this gift from a master teacher who weekly challenges hundreds of women in Bellevue's Women's Ministry. Through a wealth of Scripture and lessons she has learned along the way, she has captured the essence of the journey necessary to move from the natural to the supernatural—to the More!"

Marge Lenow
Director of Women's Ministry,
Bellevue Baptist Church, Cordova, Tennessee

"With a divine passion and clarity, Donna Gaines invites women to live lives in the 'More.' From her own personal walk, she has experienced living life from the 'inside out' and challenges the reader to capture the vision that our heavenly Father has had for us since the beginning of time. I highly recommend this book for any woman desiring to capture the 'more' you've always been missing!"

Diane Nix
Speaker, Author, and Seminary Professor's Wife
New Orleans, Louisiana

"Donna Gaines has done all of us a service by writing this biblical, practical book on the Holy Spirit. The best thing about this work is that Donna lives what she teaches."

Barbara O'Chester
Speaker and Wife of Harold O'Chester,
Pastor Emeritus, Great Hills Baptist Church, Austin, Texas

"How needed. A practical book on enjoying the Spirit-filled life. How appropriate. A book on the subject written by a godly pastor's wife who demonstrates a Spirit-filled life in her own daily walk with the Lord. Read this book with profit. How wonderful!"

Jerry Vines
Pastor Emeritus, First Baptist Church, Jacksonville, Florida;
Two-time President, Southern Baptist Convention;
President, Jerry Vines Ministries, Inc.

THERE'S GOTTA BE MORE!

Enjoying THE SPIRIT–FILLED LIFE

THERE'S GOTTA BE MORE!

Donna Gaines

B&H
PUBLISHING GROUP

Nashville, Tennessee

ISBN: 978-0-8054-4440-7

Published by B&H Publishing Group,
Nashville, Tennessee

Dewey Decimal Classification: 248.843
Subject Heading: CHRISTIAN LIFE \ WOMEN

Unless otherwise noted, all Scripture quotations are taken from the Holman Christian Standard Bible˚ copyright © 1999, 2000, 2002, 2003 by Holman Bible Publishers. Used by permission. Holman Christian Standard Bible˚, Holman CSB˚, and HCSB˚ are federally registered trademarks of Holman Bible Publishers.

Other Bibles quoted are marked AMP, Amplified Bible, copyright © 1954, 1958, 1962, 1964, 1965, 1987 by The Lockman Foundation; MSG, *The Message,* copyright © 1993, 1994, 1995, 1996, 2000, 2001, 2002 by Eugene H. Peterson; NASB, New American Standard Bible, copyright © 1960, 1962, 1963, 1968, 1971, 1972, 1973, 1975, 1977, 1995 by The Lockman Foundation; NIV, New International Version, copyright © 1973, 1978, 1984 by International Bible Society; NKJV, New King James Version, copyright © 1982 by Thomas Nelson, Inc.; NLT, Holy Bible, New Living Translation copyright © 1996, 2004 by Tyndale Charitable Trust, used by permission of Tyndale House Publishers.

1 2 3 4 5 6 7 8 9 10 11 12 13 14 15   12 11 10 09 08

This book is dedicated to my husband Steve.
When I met you during our college days,
you sparked a hunger in my soul to walk in the Spirit.
I saw in you what I had longed for. What a privilege it is
to be your life partner in marriage and ministry.
I love you!

Contents

Foreword   xi

Acknowledgments   xv

Introduction   1

1—Is That All There Is?   5

2—You Can Run but You Cannot Hide   11

3—To Tell the Truth   21

4—Why Settle for Less?   29

5—I Give Up!   39

6—How about a Love Checkup?   53

7—Where the Battle Is Won   61

8—Off with the Old!   71

9—On with the New!   83

10—God Fixes Broken Things   91

11—Know Your Enemy   103

12—Forgiveness Is a Choice   115

13—It's Not about Me!   125

14—The Downward Spiral   135

15—The Power of the Spoken Word (Part 1)   145

16—The Power of the Spoken Word (Part 2)   153

17—The Lure of the Supernatural   163

Contents

18—Purity Begins Within   169

19—Run to Win!   179

20—It's about Time   185

21—Follow Me As I Follow Christ   193

22—Cheering Us On!   199

Works Consulted and Quoted   203

Foreword

As I finished the last page of this book, tears welled up in my eyes and my heart cried out, "I am unworthy to write the foreword to this book." After teaching prayer and living Jesus virtually around the clock in ministry for more than forty of my now eighty-five years, I just had been alternately encouraged, confirmed, inspired, motivated, and reproved.

If you are dissatisfied with the status quo or if you have been knowingly or subconsciously longing for *More*, here is a book that, if faithfully practiced step-by-step, actually will give it to you. And surprisingly, it also will be what God has been desiring for you all along.

Donna has not only researched but for many years has practiced the two secrets of her journey for this book on *More:* Jesus and the written Word of God. Applying both only can be from the Holy Spirit filling and controlling us from the inside out, not from some external influence on our minds and bodies.

First, Jesus. Coming out of her own quest for *More* was a new intimacy, relationship, and walk with Him. She weaves the awesome BC (before Christ) lessons and history in the Old Testament into the New Testament's AD (after Jesus) marching orders for God's children. This AD change came about through Jesus's coming, shedding His blood for our sins, being resurrected, ascending back to His Father in heaven, sending the Holy Spirit to dwell in us, and promising His return in glory and power.

Suddenly, you will discover the only Source for quenching that longing for *More* is not found in things or circumstances, but in a Person—Jesus! Donna has us step back and get a panoramic view of world history, starting with creation of the two first humans who began by having *Everything*. Then when Adam and Eve chose to sin, all humans fell into a state of sin, desperately needing something *More*. But the Father knew when it was time to send our something *More*, to reestablish that intimate relationship—not just for priests and prophets but for us all to be eligible to go individually right into the Holy of Holies with the God of the universe through the blood of our *More*—Jesus!

Second, God's Word. Donna Gaines's longing for *More* in her life produced what is also the kind of life Jesus desires for all of His followers. Her discernment and insight into the Word of God will open potential for spiritual growth in you that you never dreamed was even there for the taking. The steps are not always easy but gradually, in giant strides or little baby steps, people will see—and you will know—you really *do* have something *More!*

The power of this book for me was Donna's extensive use of Scripture itself, which, after all, is the only truth we can rely on. It is profound yet readable. Sprinkled with enough human and biblical stories to avoid being merely dry theology, the book exudes her passion for the Bible and its author God Himself.

This is not merely a "head knowledge" book, but a body, soul, and spirit-permeating instrument that, when honestly applied, actually changes the reader's outlook and lifestyle. It brims with the author's own life lessons as she let God use His Word as a mirror to see herself as He sees her—and then shares the victorious answers He has taught her, also right out of His Word.

There is one chapter that is a rare gem—it extensively covers awesome new thoughts and methods that produce the joy and life-changing rewards of meeting God first in each day. It all starts with "It's about Time" for setting aside a place and a time for God through His Word, the Bible, and then continues with an incredible array of potential next steps she has practiced and recommends. The whole book is worth just this one chapter.

This book should be, will be, recognized as a *classic* of living the Christian life in this period of our history—with our *More*—Jesus.

Evelyn Christenson
Evelyn Christenson Ministries
St. Paul, Minnesota

Acknowledgments

Very special thanks are due to those who helped make this work a reality. My journey with Christ began when I was nine years old. Since that time, the Lord has allowed me to cross paths with some incredible men and women of God. This book is a composition of the many people the Lord has used to point me to Him and cause me to desire to walk in the fullness of His Spirit. Thank you, Dad and Mom, for raising me in a Christian home and for being such great examples of servants of the Lord. Thank you to the two greatest sisters in the world: Lisa and Julie. Not only are you my sisters; you are my friends and spiritual confidants. You spur me on in my pursuit of Christ.

A great big thanks to my family. Steve, you have encouraged me and believed in the Lord's calling on my life. I couldn't have done this without your support and encouragement. To my children—our son, Grant, and his wife, Melisa, and our daughters, Lindsey, Allison, and Bethany; how could any mother have more wonderful children? I have often told you I marvel that the Lord has allowed me to be the mother of such incredible human beings! What a joy it is to see you growing up and becoming the men and women the Lord has created you to be.

Thank you Diane for being such a special friend and fellow-pursuer of Christ in every season of our lives. You have sharpened me.

Thank you to the members of the Women's Ministry of First Baptist Church in Gardendale, Alabama, who were a part of this Bible study's coming into being. Thank you to Charlotte, Dianne, and Pam for praying until God birthed the women's ministry. The Lord granted us the blessing of growing together in Him: Bible studies, conferences, retreats, mission trips—you are each on every page of this book. Dayna, Joni, Pam, and Robbie: thanks for all the behind-the-scenes work and for the fun in the Women's Ministry office. Dayna and Joni, thanks especially for all the proofing and your invaluable input into this book. You are both incredible!

To Len Goss, John Landers, and George Williams from B&H who pursued this book and believed in it even before I did: thank you for allowing me to put my life message into a book.

Carolyn Goss, thank you for all of your editorial experience and expertise. You truly helped take the transcripts of the Bible study sessions and make them come alive. What a joy it has been to work with you. Thank you for your friendship!

And to the women of Bellevue Baptist Church with whom the Lord has granted me the privilege of journeying now: what a joy and honor to serve our Lord alongside you. You have been an example to all in your ministry to women. As the Lord is expanding our borders—India and beyond—may we continue to walk in the Spirit and listen and obey. The world is on His heart; can anything less be on ours?

Special thanks to Evelyn Christenson for writing the foreword. Evelyn has had a tremendous impact on my life through her own writings. She discipled me from afar. I read all of her books, attended her conferences, and had her lead "What Happens When Women Pray" at our church in Alabama. She is a champion of the faith.

Thank you. I love you all!

May His kingdom come and His will be done through the power of His Spirit!

Introduction

Our family recently moved to a new city after fourteen years in a town and community that we all loved. Though the transition has been difficult, the Lord made it very clear to us that He was calling us to this new place of service. Nonetheless, the call did not erase the pain in our hearts as we said good-bye to longtime friends and church members who had become like family.

In a whirlwind of activities right before we moved, my son graduated from college on a Saturday, my oldest daughter graduated from high school the next Thursday, and my son married his beautiful bride two days later. Whew! Talk about an emotional roller coaster! As if that were not enough, my husband was in charge of our denomination's annual pastors' conference and I was coordinating a session for pastors' wives that was to be held two weeks after the wedding. All of this while we were diligently seeking God's will in regards to the move to a new city and to the wonderful church that my husband now pastors.

I recently found a journal entry from the first weeks after our move:

I am in our new home today, sitting in my office that still has boxes and papers strewn on the floor. I stayed home this morning to work on a proposal for a book and to wait while the cable man came to hook up our cable, the air conditioner repairman came to repair a unit that isn't working, and an ice machine was delivered. The cable guy came first. Even though they had dug a trench in our yard and our neighbors' yard (cutting their electric dog fence) to lay the line, he was unable to connect it. This is the third time I have been here to meet someone who was unable to complete the job. The ice machine needs a place to drain, so a plumber must be called. The air conditioning repairman wrote the day down wrong. Will tomorrow be OK?

The next day's entry:

The air-conditioning repairman came today. I may as well laugh to keep from crying. He checked the unit in the attic and wanted to check the ones outside. I followed him out. When I tried to reenter the house, I realized the door had locked. The people who had lived in our house before had put padlocks on the gates of the fence, which we had not yet removed. I was locked out of my house and in the backyard with the air-conditioning repairman! I looked at this man, who was younger than I am, and said, "One of us is going to have to climb the fence." He stated very matter-of-factly that he had a bad knee. So here I go, up and over the fence. I walked around to the front of my house where the door was standing wide open! Such is life on this side of Eden!

Honestly answer these questions: What do you do with the frustrations of life? How do you handle disappointment? What about the constant nagging feeling that life was supposed to be better than this? What do you do with the recurring thought that there must be more to life than you are experiencing?

We all want more. As children we wanted more cookies, more toys, or more gifts at Christmas. As teenagers we wanted more freedom, more popularity, more time—a later curfew. In college I began longing for a different kind of more—more of the Spirit, a more abundant life, more of Jesus.

My husband, Steve, and I started dating in college. A handsome football player who had transferred to the college I attended, he was a new Christian, and what really drew me to him was his passion for Christ. As we were getting to know each other, he asked me one day, "Donna, what do you want out of life?"

And immediately I knew. I said, "I want more than the status quo. Steve, there has got to be more to the Christian life than I have experienced."

Now don't get me wrong. I grew up in a great Christian home and in a wonderful church, but I knew in my heart there was a way to know God more intimately—I wanted to walk with Him, hear His voice, and commune with Him moment by moment of every day. I wanted to know how to do this. I wanted to experience the Lord in His fullness.

That desire remains in me today.

God has made me increasingly aware that my calling is to help other women learn the principles and practice of a life of knowing and experiencing God. Not long ago I was trying to decide what I was going to call the topical Bible study I was preparing to lead on how to have this deeper, more fulfilling relationship with Christ. As Steve and I rode around one day taking care of some errands, I talked to him about it.

"I don't want a churchy name for the study," I told him.

"Donna, four or five times you have said, 'There's gotta be more.' That's what you need to go with."

I thought, *Lord, that's it; that really is it. There's Gotta Be More!*

1
Is That All There Is?

*I have come that they may have life
and have it in abundance.*
JOHN 10:10b

As you stand in the checkout line at your neighborhood grocery, do you ever find yourself thumbing through any of the
glossy magazines with covers that scream at you, enticing you to
buy the magazine so you can read about ways to get more out of
life? Recently these headlines tried to grab my attention:

> *"The #1 Get-Slim Cardio Plan"*
> *"Treat Yourself Right—You Deserve It"*
> *"How to Fake Flawless Skin"*
> *"The Take Charge Guide—Smart Ways
>   to Get What You Really Want"*
> *"Legs You'll Love in Only Eight Minutes a Day"*
> *"Making Anger Work for You"*
> *"Fashion Must-Haves"*
> *"Look Great at Any Age! 36 Style Secrets That Work"*

The magazine headlines in the grocery racks are examples of some of the ways our culture says we can get more out of life. We see images of women starving themselves to the point of death, having affairs, divorcing their husbands, and having their bodies sculpted by plastic surgeons. When those things don't work, they become addicted to drugs, alcohol, sex, food, or even thrills.

So what is our culture demanding of us as women? We need to be more physically fit. We have to look good. We must have flawless skin. We need to have sex appeal. We need to be wearing the latest fashions. And yet when we take the advice of the magazines, we end up running in circles, unsatisfied, feeling as if we don't measure up and wanting to give up.

I suspect that most Christians go through days when we think, *This can't be all there is to life!* Our minds tell us, *This isn't really living,* and our hearts cry out, *There's got to be more to life than this*—and there is!

How do I know? Let's go back to the very beginning of time and visit God's original plan.

We Were Created for More[1]

Genesis 1:26–27 is a statement about God's original plan for us: "Then God said, 'Let Us make man in Our image according to Our likeness. They will rule over the fish of the sea, the birds of the sky, the animals, all the earth, and the creatures that crawl on the earth.' So God created man in His own image; He created him in the image of God; He created them male and female."

When Steve and I were expecting our first child, we imagined who he or she would be like. Would he have Steve's big brown

---

1. Throughout this book, *More* (sometimes "the More") will be capitalized for emphasis. The word *less* will not be capitalized, even when it appears in contrast to "More."

eyes, or would she have my wild curly hair? Our firstborn was a son, and he looked just like his father. After pregnancy, morning sickness, and a difficult labor, I wasn't sure I liked that! People would see him for the first time and say, "He is the spitting image of his father." Grant is now an adult and his looks and mannerisms are, in fact, very much like his father's.

In the same way that my son is an image of his father, we were created as images of our heavenly Father. In His original plan we were designed to look like God. But is it only our physical appearance that God had in mind? I don't think so. Let me explain.

God is a trichotomy. A trichotomy has three parts. God is Father, Son, and Holy Spirit—what we refer to as the Trinity. Because we are created in His image, we are also a trichotomy—a spirit, soul, and body. Our *spirit,* our inner man, comes first. The inner man is the part of our being that has the capacity to know God. Next comes our *soul*—our mind, our will, and our emotions. Third, our *body* with its five senses is how we encounter the physical world.

God uniquely crafted us with a definite plan in mind. Look at the diagram. It is a picture of life lived in the Spirit—from the inside out.

We Were Created for Relationship

We were created to live life from our spirit to the *outside* and to be in constant communion and oneness with our Father. He desired for us to know Him intimately with no barriers to separate us.

Life in the Garden of Eden is a picture of what it means to live life from the inside out. The security and intimacy of our spirit relationship with God was intended to define our lives. What did Adam and Eve experience?

- They experienced *intimacy* with the Father. They knew Him and He knew them. They were able to experience the love of God and love for each other. God literally walked with them in the garden.
- They experienced *security.* There was absolutely no fear, no anxiety, and no worry. The Father protected them and met their every need.
- They experienced *innocence and purity* in their relationship with the Lord and in their relationship with each other. Scripture tells us they were naked, but they felt no shame in their nakedness (Gen. 2:25). There was no reason to hide.

But something happened that changed everything. Sin entered the garden. "Now the serpent [Satan] was the most cunning of all the wild animals that the LORD God had made. He said to the woman, 'Did God really say, "You can't eat from any tree in the garden"?' The woman said to the serpent, 'We may eat the fruit from the trees in the garden. But about the fruit of the tree in the middle of the garden, God said, "You must not eat it or touch it, or you will die"'" (Gen. 3:1–3).

Satan cast doubt on God's command, and then he blatantly denied God's Word. "'No! You will not die,' the serpent said to the woman. 'In fact, God knows that when you eat it your eyes will be opened and you will be like God, knowing good and evil'" (Gen. 3:4–5). The serpent was telling her that God was holding out on her. With well-crafted questions, Satan planted seeds of dissatisfaction in Eve's heart. She began to view the garden differently. Instead of seeing a place of abundance and plenty that God had provided, all she could see was the single tree that she was unable to enjoy. Eve then began to doubt God's goodness: "Then the woman saw that the tree was good for food and delightful to look at, and that it was desirable for obtaining wisdom. So she took some of its fruit and ate [it]; she also gave [some] to her husband, [who was] with her, and he ate [it]. Then the eyes of both of them were opened, and they knew that they were naked; so they sewed fig leaves together and made loincloths for themselves" (Gen. 3:6–7).

Sin Created Separation

Our natural response to sin is to hide. Guilt and shame compel us to hide from God. But God won't leave us in hiding. He relentlessly pursues us. "Then the man and his wife heard the sound of the LORD God walking in the garden at the time of the evening breeze, and they hid themselves from the LORD God among the trees of the garden. So the LORD God called out to the man and said to him, 'Where are you?'" (Gen. 3:9).

For this couple who had never experienced any negative emotions, the crushing weight of fear, shame, and guilt sent them running from God. Adam was afraid, so he hid and blamed his sin on the woman that God had given him. Eve, in turn, blamed the serpent.

Adam and Eve fell from God's original design and could no longer live from the inside out. We also suffered spiritual death and ultimately physical death because of their sin.

We Began to Live Life Backward, from the Outside In

After the fall we began to filter everything through our physical senses, our emotions, and our minds—instead of being defined by the Spirit. We lost the communion we had experienced with God.

- We lost intimacy, and we now experience separation.
- We lost security, and we now experience fear.
- We lost innocence, and we now experience guilt and shame.

Wow—we had everything perfect in the garden. But because of sin and willful disobedience, it's all gone. All of us have fallen from the More that the Lord had prepared for us. We miss, long for, and grieve over the perfect life of security we've lost. We grieve because we're supposed to. We grieve because of the life we lost through sin. It is this life—living from the inside out—that we spend all of our days longing to regain.

One of the most destructive lies of the enemy is that there is no way back. Or that maybe God allows some people to experience intimacy with Him, but it certainly couldn't be for us personally. Yet God is still asking us the same question He asked Adam and Eve: "Where are you?"

Are you in hiding? Have you run for cover?

Listen closely now. Feel the cool breeze of the garden as the Father calls your name. He is in pursuit.

2

You Can Run but You Cannot Hide

Where can I go to escape Your Spirit?
How can I flee from Your presence?
PSALM 139:7

When my children were toddlers, they loved to play hide-and-seek with a towel or even a napkin in a restaurant. When their eyes were covered and they couldn't see me, they assumed that I couldn't see them. I would play along and squeal with delight when they uncovered their faces as though they had just been "found"!

When Adam and Eve realized they had sinned, they ran for cover. They created their own covering with fig leaves, constructed to conceal their guilt and shame. They hid themselves from God because they were ashamed of how they looked and of what they had done. They hid from each other because they were now so aware of themselves that they were self-conscious.

All of us are in hiding until we meet Jesus. But our covering is as futile as fig leaves or the napkin my children hid behind.

We all feel lost, separated, fearful, and consumed with guilt and shame. We, too, fell from all that God had originally created and designed us to be. We fell from the possibility of *More*—a coveted relationship in which we had been promised not only deep friendship but deeper intimacy and communion with God.

And just like Adam and Eve, we also construct coverings. This desire to cover is what lures us to the answers our culture provides. Unfortunately, these answers are no better than the sewn fig leaves of Adam and Eve. They cover no better and do nothing to eliminate our pain—pain that is caused by our separation from God and those with whom He created us to relate.

God not only pursued Adam and Eve after their sin, but He also provided a covering for them. Genesis 3:21 tells us that an animal had to die, quite literally, for them to be covered: "The LORD God made clothing out of skins for Adam and his wife." Once He covered them, God then drove them from the garden, preventing them from eating from the Tree of Life and separating them from Him forever. However, He also put in motion a plan to bring them back at great cost to Himself.

With Separation Came Spiritual Death

When the human race became disobedient to God, we died spiritually. Because of our sin, we are no longer able to live primarily from the spirit outward. As a consequence, our soul and body take primacy over the spirit, and we live life filtered through our senses. As the next diagram shows, like Eve, we elevate our own reasoning above the Word of God and live life backward.

When we live life backward, from the outside in, our identity is no longer defined by the safety and security of a relation-

ship with God. Our identity
is defined more from our
outside appearance, our per-
ception of what others think
about us, and our feelings.
Our body and soul conspire
to tell us that a relationship

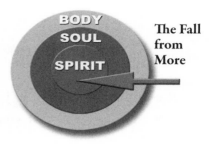

with God is not possible—we feel either that we are not good
enough to enter into a relationship with Him or we give up,
determining that God cannot be known.

Yes, we humans fell from the More that God had created for
us. But the good news is that we have been saved *for* More. We
have been saved for More through Jesus Christ. When we receive
Christ into our lives, we are born again (John 3). Our spirit is
regenerated and the Spirit of God
comes to live within our spirit.
He takes up residence in our
inner person. Look at the cross in
the next diagram and note how
it covers the new believer's spirit,
freeing it to point outward.

Through Jesus Our Trichotomy Is Restored to Its God-Designed Order

Jesus of Nazareth came to restore what was lost in the fall.
First Peter 2:24 tells us, "He Himself bore our sins in His body on
the tree." Our sins, all of them, were paid for in full on that crudely
constructed cross at Calvary. That means that every wrong we have
ever done and every wrong thing we ever will do has already been

13

accounted for, bar none. We can boldly come before God's throne to receive grace and mercy to help in time of need (Heb. 4:16). We can come before Him in repentance and confession and have our sins completely washed away (1 John 1:9).

Romans 5:8 tells us that "while we were still sinners, Christ died for us!" That means that while we were still in hiding, creating our own coverings, Christ died. Just as an animal had to die to cover Adam and Eve, Jesus had to die to cover us. He not only died to cover us; He died to give us life as it was intended. He has once again made it possible for us to experience intimacy, security, and purity.

The apostle Paul describes our new status this way: "Therefore if any man is in Christ, he is a new creature; the old things passed away; behold, new things have come" (2 Cor. 5:17 NASB). The old way of living life from the outside in, the old way of having fallen from the More that God created us to experience, is no longer to be our lot in life. We are to once again live from the inside out in fullness of relationship with the God of the universe.

First Corinthians 2:9–10 describes what the Father has given us through Jesus Christ: "'Things which eye has not seen and ear has not heard, and which have not entered the heart of man, all that God has prepared for those who love Him.' For to us God revealed them through the Spirit" (NASB). The original word for "revealed" in this passage, *apokalupto,* has within it the word *kalupto,* which refers to veiling, hiding, or covering. The word suggests unveiling and, in the context of this verse, to make known a thing previously unknown.

What does this mean for us? Jesus has removed the veil of separation. God has opened our hearts and minds to His Spirit and the truths He reveals. He begins to reveal Himself to us as we walk in obedience. His Spirit bears witness with our spirit that we are children of God (Rom. 8:16). He begins to reveal in our Spirit-man (the innermost part of our being) what He has prepared for us.

In 1 Corinthians 2:10b–13 Paul writes, "For the Spirit searches everything, even the deep things of God. For who among men knows the concerns of a man except the spirit of the man that is in him? In the same way, no one knows the concerns of God except the Spirit of God. Now we have not received the spirit of the world, but the Spirit who is from God."[1]

Paul describes three types of people in 1 Corinthians 2 and 3. There is the spiritual man (living life from the inside out, as God has planned it, "created for More"), the natural man (not yet having accepted the person of Christ and thus living life from the outside in, "fallen from More"), and the carnal one (a Christian but still living life from the outside in, in a state of "less than More").

We who are living as spiritual people have not been given the spirit of the world—we have been given the *Spirit of God.* In our new relationship with God, His Spirit now resides within our inner person, in our spirit. As our Friend, He is revealing to us not just God's will and not just who God is. He does those things, but even more intimately, He reveals to us the very thoughts of God—in our inner person, through our own spirit, and not just with human words.

Let me try to put this passage into terms we all understand. I have a very dear, very close girlfriend. Though we know each

---

1. A quick differentiation between "spirit" and "Spirit" as they appear in this book: When capitalized, "Spirit" always refers to the Holy Spirit, the third person of the Trinity. When used without capitalization, it refers either to the inner person or to a prevailing tone or attitude in the world itself. Similarly, phrases such as "spiritually discerned" refer to human reactions or activity related to the inward person, while "Spirit eyes," "Spirit-man," and similar terms refer to qualities or concepts directly traceable back to the Holy Spirit Himself as He works within the Christian.

other really well and can almost complete each other's sentences, the only way I can be sure what she is thinking is if she chooses to tell me. Most of the time she does because we're close friends. The limitation is that we, as humans, must use words to reveal our thoughts to each other.

Paul explains the difference between human discourse and conversation with God: "which things we also speak, not in words taught by human wisdom, but in those taught by the Spirit, combining spiritual thoughts with spiritual words. But a natural man does not accept the things of the Spirit of God, for they are foolishness to him; and he cannot understand them, because they are spiritually appraised" (1 Cor. 2:13–14 NASB).

The natural man (fallen from More) is the second person Paul describes. Have you ever tried to share a spiritual truth with a friend or family member only to see them look blankly at you as if you were speaking another language, or as if they can't hear what you're saying? If you try to share a spiritual truth with someone who doesn't have a relationship with Christ and the person doesn't understand, there is a reason. He cannot understand because he (or she) is a natural man. Unless you have the Holy Spirit living within you, you cannot understand spiritual things. Paul says that the spiritual person has been given the very mind of Christ (1 Cor. 2:16 NASB).

Why Do We Choose the Flesh?

In spite of all we have for the asking, Paul explains: "And I, brethren, could not speak to you as to spiritual men, but as to men of flesh, as to infants in Christ. I gave you milk to drink, not solid food; for you were not yet able to receive it. Indeed, even now you are not yet able, for you are still fleshly. For since there is jealousy and strife among you, are you not fleshly, and are you not walking like mere men?" (1 Cor. 3:1–3 NASB).

The *carnal* Christian, the growth-stunted Christian—the Christian ruled by the flesh (soul and body) rather than by the Spirit—is the third person Paul discusses in this passage. Regrettably, this is where most Christians live. We do not walk in the fullness and maturity of all that Christ purchased for us by His death on the cross.

Why? We have been deceived. The enemy has clouded and darkened our reasoning, causing us to elevate our own thinking above the Word of God. When we revert to the flesh, we are returning to what is familiar, to our comfort zone. In addition, we ourselves have willfully chosen to disobey in many areas of life. When we do that, we open the door to the enemy, and we quench the flow of God's precious Spirit, limiting what He desires to do through us and in us. Not only that, but we limit our relationship with God.

We were meant for More. We were meant to know God's very thoughts. He desires to reveal Himself to us. So why do most of us live like a carnal Christian? We are living in less than More, settling for so much less than what Jesus Christ died to give us. The following diagram shows the status of the carnal Christian, when once again the body and the soul overpower the spirit.

Paul expressed his concern about the Christian who remains in a carnal, immature condition: "But I fear that, as the serpent deceived Eve by his

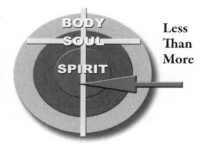

cunning, your minds may be corrupted from a complete and pure devotion to Christ" (2 Cor. 11:3). The carnal person is not Spirit-driven and Spirit-controlled but is controlled by his or her flesh. To paraphrase Paul's words, he is saying, "I am fearful for you because I am afraid you are going to be like Eve. You are going to be easily deceived or led astray from the purity and the simplicity of devotion to Jesus Christ, which is what the Christian life is all about."

The Greek word for "deceived" in 2 Corinthians 11:3, *exapatao,* means "to cause someone to have false ideas about something; to beguile." Satan was presenting lies as truth, and Eve assumed the lies were reality. Because she believed the lies, her actions were based on assumed reality—on faulty facts. We must not let these false assumptions derail us as they did Eve.

Living Life from the Inside Out Leads to More

If we are not experiencing the amazing quality of life promised by Jesus, why not? Let's get honest. Many times it is because we have been living our lives based on *feelings* instead of *truth.*

Most of us as women are more sensitive to feelings—ours and those of other people. Many times I am able to sense if someone else is discouraged or stressed. That intuitive knowing is a gift from God. But as with every one of God's gifts, Satan seeks to come in and pervert and distort what God created to be good. As a consequence, we can become feelings-driven instead of truth-driven. When that happens, we are allowing ourselves to become double-minded (a man or woman of divided allegiance) and unstable in all our ways (James 1:8). Our decisions must be based on truth, not on our feelings.

How do we change those behavior patterns? How do we tear down the deceptions, unveiling and exposing the lies of the enemy so we can replace them with the truth of God's Word?

We do it by choosing to act on what we know is true. When we do that, our feelings will eventually line up. We must be truth-driven and not feelings-driven. In the words of Colossians 3:1, we must set our mind on "what is above," not on earthly things. We must look forward and keep our eyes on Jesus (Heb. 12:2).

We can choose to submit to God daily, communing with Him and allowing Him to "interrupt" our days. When we do that, what will happen? We will come to the end of our pursuits as Jesus did and be able to say, "I brought glory to you here on earth by completing the work you gave me to do" (John 17:4 NLT). How awesome! One of these days each of us is going to face the Lord. It could be a short time from now, or it could be many years away. When I face Him, I want to be found faithful. I do not want to have missed out on anything God had for me on this side of heaven. Jesus said in John 10:10, "I have come that they may have life and have it in abundance," and that means *now,* not just in eternity.

I ask you the question God asked Adam and Eve: Where are you? Do you have a relationship with God? If not, He invites you to commit your life completely to Jesus, asking Him to forgive your sins and be your Savior. He will forgive you, save you, and fill you with His Spirit. He is the only One who can restore you to the relationship that God originally intended.

If you have never committed your life to Christ and would like to, you can stop right now and ask Him to save you. Simply pray something like this from your heart:

Dear Heavenly Father,

I know that I am a sinner. I am separated from You. I ask You to forgive me of my sins and to save me. Thank You for Your salvation. Please fill me with Your Spirit and help me to live life from the inside out from this day forward.

In Jesus's name, Amen.

If you already have a relationship with God through Jesus Christ, are you living out the reality of a Spirit-controlled life? Or have you been deceived, allowing faulty feelings to rule your life instead of God's Spirit?

You don't have to figure everything out before you choose to follow Christ wholeheartedly, but you do need to choose. This is the choice we must all make. It is after we take that first step of faith that He begins to reveal Himself to us so that the truths of the Bible make sense and come alive.

Once we've made the choice to follow Christ, we *will* encounter the enemy. The same serpent that ambushed Eve is accosting us as well. The only way to discern his deception is to know the truth.

3

To Tell the Truth

You will know the truth, and the truth will set you free.
JOHN 8:32

When I was in the third grade, I had a wonderful Sunday school teacher, Mrs. Goodman. She challenged us to memorize the books of the Bible and also specific Scriptures. She rewarded us with gifts and prizes. Because of her instruction and encouragement, I can still recite the books of the Bible and the verses I memorized when I was nine years old. As I have meditated on those verses through the years, they have become a part of me.

To Expose Satan's Lies, We Must Know the Truth

Knowing and memorizing Scripture is essential. We should always ask: What does Scripture say? "You will know the truth, and the truth will set you free" (John 8:32). It is the truth we *know* both intellectually and experientially that becomes a part of who we are. Then we must ask: How does it apply to me?

The serpent's lies to us are the same ones he used with Eve in the garden. He begins by tempting us to doubt the Word of God.

Then he blatantly denies God's Word and casts doubt on God's goodness. When we give in to the temptation as Eve did, then fear, guilt, shame, and all of those other emotions come crashing in. Like Eve, we begin to believe more lies about God. I call them "deadly lies" because they distort and pervert the truth, leading us to choose death instead of life.

Deadly Lies

The following are some of the most common:

Lie #1: God Is Holding Out on You

"He can't be trusted. You must take control." That is what the serpent told Eve. The same words are hissed into our ears today. The truth is that the Lord desires to bless and reveal Himself to His children.

Lie #2: God Is Distant

"He wound the world up and He let it go." A song that was popular a few years ago stated: "God is watching us from a distance." Somebody told me that she had heard that song sung in a church service. In a church service! This is not the God revealed in the Bible! God is not distant. He interacts with us in our innermost beings, beside us and with His Holy Spirit in us, to bring about His will and to make us more like Jesus. Psalm 139 describes God's deep, all-encompassing love for us: "LORD, You have searched me and known me. You know when I sit down and when I stand up; You understand my thoughts from far away. . . . You are aware of all my ways. Before a word is on my tongue, You know all about it, LORD. . . . Where can I go to escape Your Spirit? Where can I flee from Your presence? If I go up to heaven,

You are there; if I make my bed in Sheol, You are there. . . . Even the darkness is not dark to You" (vv. 1–12).

Lie #3: God Has No Purpose for Your Life

"You were merely an accident." This is not what Scripture tells us! Psalm 139 continues, "For it was You who created my inward parts; You knit me together in my mother's womb" (v. 13).

Whatever the circumstances were surrounding your birth, you were planned by the Creator God, and He formed you and put you together. If God formed you, created you, and gave you life, He has a purpose for you—and it is for your good and for the good of His kingdom. "I will praise You, because I have been remarkably and wonderfully made. Your works are wonderful, and I know [this] very well. My bones were not hidden from You when I was made in secret, when I was formed in the depths of the earth. Your eyes saw me when I was formless; all [my] days were written in Your book and planned before a single one of them began. God, how difficult Your thoughts are for me [to comprehend]; how vast their sum is! If I counted them, they would outnumber the grains of sand; when I wake up, I am still with You" (Ps. 139:14–18).

God the Creator is thinking about you every moment of every day! He loves you, and He is intimately acquainted with every part of you. After all, He made you!

Lie #4: God Is Harsh and Critical

Scripture tells us differently—it says that God is love. Jesus describes the Father's love in John 3:16: "For God so loved the world that he gave his one and only Son, that whoever believes in him shall not perish but have eternal life" (NIV). The enemy tells us that God has a list of things He expects from us and that

He is up in heaven watching us, ready to take us down if we don't please Him. That is not God! Anytime He disciplines us, it is for our good, to remove the things from our lives that would damage and ultimately destroy us so that we can experience the fullness of Christ. God is affirming. He is encouraging: "God's kindness is intended to lead you to repentance" (Rom. 2:4). Even His conviction is intended to restore.

Lie #5: God Is Legalistic

Legalism is adding a human list of "dos and don'ts" to God's Word and expecting everyone to follow them. We have failed as Christians because we have made the lost world think that Christianity is a bunch of rules. It isn't!

The Christian life is about relationship. It is more appropriately a list of "dos." We *do* know who He is, and we *do* have the opportunity to experience the fullness of all we can have and be in Jesus Christ.

Rules without relationship equal rebellion. It is true in the home if you are parenting children, especially teenagers, but it is also true in our relationship with the Father. If we just try to obey the rules without experiencing the relationship, we will rebel every time. When I focus on the rules instead of the Ruler, I lose my joy and become burdened with keeping the rules, adding new rules, and teaching the rules. But if I focus on the Ruler, with my greatest desire being to know Him and enjoy Him forever, I will find all that my thirsty, weary heart has longed for.

For a Christian, the key to finding More is a relationship. It is a oneness, an intimacy that God desires for us to experience with Him. I can tell you from experience that intimacy with Him and the joy it brings into my life are truly too beautiful for words. If you have ever tasted the ecstasy of the joy of His presence, there is no turning back. You will give up anything. You will be like the man who went and sold everything he owned to purchase the pearl of great price. Jesus is that pearl, and knowing Him and experiencing Him is worth everything!

Lie #6: God Is Never Satisfied

We can never measure up; we can never be good enough. And after all, didn't Jesus say, "But you are to be perfect, even as your Father in heaven is perfect" (Matt. 5:48 NLT)?

Yes, but Scripture doesn't tell us to do it in our own strength. Throughout the New Testament God says, "Come to Me surrendered in your wretchedness; let Me wash you and cleanse you and give you the righteousness of My Son. Let me fill you with My Holy Spirit so that My holiness will flow through you." We are accepted. Christ accepted us.

Zephaniah 3:17 is a small, obscure verse in the Old Testament, but its words are full of power and encouragement: "The LORD your God is in your midst, a victorious warrior. He will exult over you with joy, He will be quiet in His love, He will rejoice over you with shouts of joy" (NASB), or as the NIV puts it, "with singing."

If you are a mother, think back to the days when your babies were infants. You may have rocked them before you put them to bed, and many of you, even if you are like me and really can't sing, might have sung to your children. You sang over them.

I sang to mine. I had a little medley of songs and hymns that I would sing to them. Each of my four children, when they began to talk, could sing those songs because they had heard them so many times. I also sang over them because I rejoiced over them— I delighted in them.

I remember coming back from Israel after our first trip there. As I sat in the plane journaling about what we had seen and experienced, I began to think about our children, who would be waiting for us at the airport, and how excited I was to see them. I thought of how much I had missed them and how much I had to tell them. My heart was so full! Suddenly the Lord impressed upon me, "Donna, as excited as you are to see your children, I delight over you even more than that. It thrills Me when you come into my presence. I have so much I want to share with you, so many blessings I want to pour out on you. I delight in you."

A picture of the Father's delight is recorded in one of the Bible's most well-known stories (see Luke 15:11–32). It is a story of a son who became deluded, like Eve. He had everything he needed, but all he could see was what he didn't have. There was more to life than what he was experiencing; he was sure of it. He decided to ask for his inheritance early. He chose to dishonor his father and go his own way.

As the prodigal found out, when we choose to go our own way, the choice leads to destruction, which is according to the enemy's diabolical plan. We have two choices to make: we can choose to follow the Lord and go His way and experience life and blessing and abundance, or we can choose to go the way of our flesh, which draws us into devilish traps and schemes that lead to curses, death, and destruction (Deut. 30:19). At the time we are choosing, we don't see the whole picture. We may forget that going our own way leads to grief. We may believe the lie that we will be the one that beats the system, that we will be able to get away with it. We can handle it!

The prodigal son was just that haughty and arrogant. He had

lots of friends as long as he had money. But the money eventually ran out and he ended up feeding pigs—and the pigs were eating better than he was! Think of the humiliation—a young Jewish man feeding swine! Surrounded by the stench and grunts of pigs, he came to his senses: "How many of my father's hired hands have more than enough food, and here I am dying of hunger!" (Luke 15:17). He thought to himself, *I know what I will do, I will prepare a speech. I will go back and tell my father, "Don't take me back as a son, just take me back as a servant."*

We know what happened. He made his way home, beaten down, starving, ragged, and spent. What he didn't know was that his father had been watching for him every day, scanning that dusty horizon for the glimpse of a distant but familiar figure. When the father spotted him afar off, he recognized his son and ran toward him.

Embracing him, the father paid no attention to his son's rehearsed apologies. He commanded his servants, "Quick! Bring out the best robe and put it on him; put a ring on his finger. . . . Then bring the fattened calf. . . . This son of mine was dead and is alive again; he was lost and is found!" (vv. 22–24).

And that is what the Father does for us. At times we believe the lies of Satan, who whispers into our ears that if we have sinned, been disobedient, and fallen away from the Lord, we can't come back to Him. We end up like Adam and Eve hiding behind the bushes, so afraid that God is going to find us out, when in reality we are already laid bare before Him.

Remember the words of Psalm 139? God knows the words we are going to speak even before they are formed on our tongue. He knows everything about us. He is that Father, waiting with bated breath, watching for us to turn toward home. When we do,

He runs toward us and restores our rightful place in His family as joint heirs with Jesus Christ.

But wait a minute. There was another person in that story whose actions sometimes get glossed over. The elder brother might be a picture of today's carnal Christian. He complained, "Well, here I have been all along, faithfully working for you, never disobeying orders, and what do I get out of it?"

What did the father say to him? "You are always with me, and everything I have is yours" (Luke 15:31). While the elder brother had everything—his father's presence and all that he owned—he could not rejoice over the return of his lost brother. He had not experienced all that sonship provided. Feeling no joy in the certainty of his father's love for him, he was envious, one of the prime characteristics of living life in the flesh.

That kind of attitude is the root cause of dissention both in our families and in the family of God. Remember how Paul asked the Corinthians, "For since there is envy and strife among you, are you not fleshly and living like ordinary people?" (1 Cor. 3:3).

We might ask the same question: How can this be for those of us who have so much? We have the Word of God, we have Christian books, we have Bible studies, we can acquire reams of head knowledge, but also we need to allow God's truth to seep down into our heart and our spirit and change us from the inside out.

Maybe you're thinking, *OK, fine, but that isn't what I am experiencing; I am not walking in the abundance—the More— that Jesus Christ died to give me.* There is good news. If you will hang in there with Him, He will show you. He will reveal to you what is hindering you from experiencing More—that deeply personal relationship with Him. Each of us is faced with a choice: the truth or a lie—less or More.

4

Why Settle for Less?

Be filled with the Spirit.
EPHESIANS 5:18b

The RMS *Titanic,* the most luxurious sea vessel of its time, collided with an iceberg on April 14, 1912, and sank within two and a half hours, taking some of the most prominent citizens of the era to a watery grave. The story is told of a wealthy lady who was in her cabin when the order to abandon ship was given. Having no time to pack her belongings, she noticed two things on her dressing table—her jewel box full of expensive jewelry and a bowl of oranges. Knowing she could only take what would fit in her pockets, she abandoned her diamonds and pearls and quickly grabbed some oranges. The value of the life-sustaining oranges far exceeded that of her jewelry collection. When faced with death, she chose that which would give life.

The Bible says, "For the mind-set of the flesh is death, but the mind-set of the Spirit is life and peace" (Rom. 8:6). By choosing to set our minds on the Spirit, we are choosing to live—really live. Paul prayed that the Thessalonians would experience this life: "Now may the God of peace Himself sanctify you entirely; and may your *spirit* and *soul* and *body* be preserved complete, without blame at the coming of our Lord Jesus Christ" (1 Thess. 5:23 NASB, italics mine). We are meant to be filled with the Spirit and to walk in the Spirit—this is life.

In Galatians 5:16 Paul explains that if we will walk in the Spirit, we will not carry out the deeds or the desires of the flesh. He earnestly commands us to be filled with the Spirit (Eph. 5:18). What does he mean? This kind of filling is an outpouring of the Spirit from your inner person. Scripture talks about the Holy Spirit many times as living water, saying that He (the Spirit) will well up within us as a spring of living water that flows out of us.

Because of the fleshly ways in which we live, we are not able to walk in the Spirit as God intended. The Spirit's flow is quenched, and Paul admonishes us not to live in such a way (1 Thess. 5:19 NASB). He tells us not to grieve the Spirit (Eph. 4:30 NASB).

Walking in the Spirit May Not Be Easy, but It Is Exciting

Walking in the Spirit is an everyday awareness, a moment-by-moment dependence on the Spirit of God to direct everything that we do. This awareness starts by spending time with Him. It starts by getting in the Bible, by sitting at His feet, by praying, by letting Him speak to us. As we do that, He will direct the day ahead of us. Many times as I begin to pray, I have my day's to-do list on my mind, but the Spirit interrupts those everyday thoughts and focuses me on what's important. God moves and works when we pray, when we seek Him, when we pursue Him.

My sister, Lisa, and a dear friend, Cathy[1], experienced an example of God moving in answer to prayer. Cathy's husband, Jim, was not a Christian. He was a successful businessman who was confident in his ability to have life figured out. He said he wasn't sure if there was a God and didn't really care. Although Cathy wanted to do or say the right things so Jim would become a Christian, it was only through prayer that she was able to let go and let God do the work. As she prayed for God to move in her husband's life, she experienced her own faith being strengthened.

Lisa, Cathy, and a Spirit-led neighbor began to pray beside Jim's desk chair, claiming his salvation. Lisa also gave Jim a copy of Josh McDowell's book *More Than a Carpenter.* An internationally known apologist for the Christian faith, McDowell offers a knowledgeable explanation of who Jesus really is, along with historical evidence that He is who He claimed to be. For more than eight years, Cathy earnestly prayed and pleaded with God, asking Him to surround Jim with Christians and to bring him into His kingdom.

Jim started having vision problems, which were diagnosed as a cyst behind one of his eyes. This was potentially a serious, even career-ending condition. Suddenly his world was turned upside down. But God worked through the surgeon to remove the cyst without any further complications, and it had not eroded any of the bone around the eye.

Cathy asked Jim, "Can't you see that God is answering prayer and that He is trying to get your attention?"

Soon after the surgery, the neighbor invited them to a special meeting at their church and lunch afterward. Who was speaking there? Josh McDowell. They agreed to go. Jim felt pressure to at least read the book that had been collecting

---

1. I have changed the names out of respect for their privacy.

dust on his bookshelf for two years. So he picked it up, and he spent the week reading *More Than a Carpenter*. He pulled up McDowell's Web site and then found the Web sites of atheists who were refuting McDowell's claims. Puffed up and self-satisfied, he seemed ready "to shoot for bear" the next day.

After McDowell's presentation, they went to lunch—which turned out to be not a small meal with six or eight people, as Cathy had expected, but a meal attended by forty! At first Cathy's heart fell. But just guess who the Lord put right next to Jim? Josh McDowell. And Josh began to talk to Jim, who fired questions right back at him.

After awhile, McDowell interrupted their back-and-forth. "Jim, I need somebody like you. I am working on a new project. I am writing a book. Would you consider giving me your e-mail address and let me e-mail you some of the chapters? I need someone like you; I need to be sure that I have all my bases covered. Would you be willing to help me on this project?"

Josh McDowell—or more accurately the Holy Spirit through Josh—reeled him right in! Jim said, "I would love to do that!" And before they finished the conversation, Josh looked at him and said, "Jim, you are exactly where I was before I met Jesus."

Not long after this encounter, Jim was invited to play golf. One of the foursome just happened to be the pastor of the church Jim's wife and children attended. The pastor befriended Jim and invited him to lunch. They continued to meet for several weeks. Everywhere Jim turned, God was bringing Christians across his path. It wasn't long after this that on a business trip, *Jim surrendered*. He knelt down and gave his heart to Christ. He came home a changed man!

When we pray, God responds. When we choose to seek God above all else, He reveals Himself. He begins to call into being "that which does not exist" (Rom. 4:17 NASB). God began to move and work in Jim's life when the women began to pray so that one day he would be sitting at lunch across from Josh McDowell—one of the greatest Christian apologists of our time—and that soon after, he would become friends with a Christian pastor. God began to move in the circumstances of Jim's life to bring Jim to Himself.

That is life in the Spirit. It is not settling for less, accepting things as they are. We must not be satisfied with the status quo; instead, we must go after More—everything Jesus Christ purchased for us on the Cross.

When we settle for less, we confine ourselves to life in the flesh. We walk like mere men and women, not Spirit-filled believers. What does life in the flesh look like? The New Living Translation of Galatians 5:19–21 describes the manifestations of the fleshly life: "When you follow the desires of your sinful nature, the results are very clear: sexual immorality, impurity, lustful pleasures, idolatry, sorcery, hostility, quarreling, jealousy, outbursts of anger, selfish ambition, dissension, division, envy, drunkenness, wild parties, and other sins like these." And Paul ends verse 21 with a warning: "Let me tell you again, as I have before, that anyone living that sort of life will not inherit the Kingdom of God."

Strong words to be sure. Anyone living this lifestyle does not belong to God! A Christian cannot habitually follow the desires of her sinful nature and not be miserable. And she will end up right in the middle of the discipline of God, because God will discipline

His child to draw her back to Himself. If there is no discipline and if there is no guilt over how we are living, we are not children of God (Heb. 12:8). But there's great news: "the Holy Spirit produces this kind of fruit in our lives: love, joy, peace, patience, kindness, goodness, faithfulness, gentleness, and self-control. There is no law against these things!" (Gal. 5:22–23 NLT).

Those who belong to Christ Jesus have nailed the passions and desires of their sinful nature to the cross and crucified them there. "Since we are living by the Spirit, let us follow the Spirit's leading in every part of our lives," Paul encourages us (Gal. 5:25 NLT).

If we are to follow the Holy Spirit, how are we to follow Him? The answer is simple, if not easy: by allowing Him to lead in every part of our lives.

We may not be committing sexual immorality or lusting after material things, but perhaps we are dealing with the more subtle attitudes of the heart. We may be struggling with moodiness or with being easily offended, "wearing our feelings on our sleeves" as my father would have described it. Maybe we are bound and determined to "protect our rights." Focusing on self always leads to selfish responses.

When We Put Our Own Rights, Needs, or Plans First, We Rebuke the Lord

"What about my needs?" That self-centered complaint goes way back, doesn't it? By putting our own rights or needs first, we rebuke the Lord just as Jesus's friend Martha did. Scripture tells us that Martha loved Jesus and Jesus loved Martha. So why did Martha rebuke the Lord?

I'm sure you remember the story well. Jesus had come for a meal at Mary and Martha's home (Luke 10:38–42). Mary may have been helping Martha prepare food before Jesus came, but once He arrived, Mary's focus was on the guest of honor. She chose to sit at His feet and listen. Jesus allowed her to stay with the men, which was not the custom in the Jewish culture of that time. Martha, on the other hand, who was busy and frazzled, had the audacity to complain to Jesus: "Do You not see? Do You not care that I have been left alone? Tell my sister to help me."

How it must grieve our Lord's heart when we ask similar questions: "Do You not see what's happening to *me*? Do You not care what happens to *me*?" It's all me, me, me! Then, like Martha, we demand of God, "Do something!" We put our needs first instead of turning to Him and saying, "Lord, I am Yours. I don't understand what is going on right now. I may not like what's happening, but I am asking You to show me Yourself in the midst of it."

The Lord responded to Martha with great patience. While Martha was "worried and bothered about so many things," He told her gently in verse 41 (NASB) that Mary had chosen the "one thing" that was necessary (v. 42). That "one thing" is Jesus! He reminded Martha that she had a choice. He desires for us to choose as well.

The next picture in Scripture of Mary and Martha with the Lord is in John 11, when their brother Lazarus was sick. The sisters sent for Jesus, but Jesus delayed His arrival, allowing Lazarus to die and be buried. Lazarus had been entombed for four days when Jesus arrived. Martha heard that Jesus was coming and went out to meet Him on the road. She said, "Lord, if You had been here my brother wouldn't have died" (v. 21). Implied in her statement is the doubt once again of His care. Jesus responded by assuring her that her brother would rise again. He also told her, "I am the resurrection and the life. . . . Everyone who lives and believes in Me will never die—ever. Do you believe this?" (vv. 25–26).

Martha believed and accepted the fact, in her own words, that Jesus was "the Messiah, the Son of God" (v. 27). Martha is proof that we can believe the right things and still not have a heart that is submissive to God's will.

Her sister Mary, on the other hand, had stayed in the house until Jesus called for her by name. When Martha informed Mary that the Teacher was there and was calling for her, Mary got up immediately and went out to meet Him on the road. She fell at His feet in a demonstration of submission and humility: "Lord, if You had been here, my brother would not have died!" (v. 32).

She said the same words her sister had said, but Mary received a very different response. Martha had run out with words meant to rebuke, and Jesus's response was to reveal His identity. Mary waited and submitted. Jesus's response to her? He revealed His heart—He wept.

When I read this passage, my heart was pierced with longing to know what had brought Jesus to tears. Surely it was not Lazarus's death! Jesus knew He was about to raise him from the dead. Was it grief over death and suffering? I'm sure it was, partially. But I believe it was more than that. I believe Jesus's heart was moved by the woman who was once again at His feet. Even though she made the same statement her sister had, her posture said, "Nevertheless, not my will but Thine be done." Mary was willing to trust her Savior even when she didn't understand.

Jesus went with them to the tomb. He told them to remove the stone. Martha protested, "What? Roll the stone away? He has been dead four days; he is going to stink" (see v. 38).

For the third time, there was a rebuke in her words. She might as well have said, "Is that what You are going to do? That is not what I had in mind. You know, You just didn't get here on time, God. You didn't do what I asked You to do."

And yet the Lord said to her, as He still says today in the midst of crisis, "You are about to behold the glory of the Lord" (see v. 40). Even when we rebuke the Lord with our doubting questions about His care, He responds in love. He gently reminds us to choose the one thing—Him. He reveals who He really is. Sometimes He even reveals His glory despite our questions. But, when we submit and worship as Mary did, Jesus invites us to join Him. He shares His thoughts and plans. He takes us places we never thought we could go. And He weeps at our sorrow and our obedience.

The only way you can know what God is calling you to do is to ask the Holy Spirit to reveal it to you. But He only reveals Himself to those who are obedient (John 14:21) and submissive. Mary submitted and consequently became one of the only followers of Christ to whom God had revealed the truth of the cross (see John 12).

Martha had a problem when things didn't go her way. Similarly, there are times we just need to keep our mouths shut and trust. We need to surrender our own plans, saying, "Father, meet me here in the midst of this situation. Don't change my husband, don't change my children, don't change my job, don't change my financial circumstances, don't change my house. God, change *me,* do a work in *me,* capture *my* heart, Lord, and make *me* more like Jesus." He then changes our perspective. We're no longer focused on making our situation work, but on finding God in the midst of it.

Remember Cathy from the beginning of the chapter? Cathy made the right choice. She chose to pray, to submit, and to let God work. Instead of rebuking her husband, nagging him or leaving him, she asked God to do what only He could do. And she saw His glory!

Jim is a picture of the natural man—one who lives in the flesh separated from Christ. Jim made the choice—he chose Jesus. Like the woman on the *Titanic,* Jim chose life. Drop the baubles and grab the oranges. It's time to choose!

5
I Give Up!

Therefore I urge you, brethren, by the mercies of God,
to present your bodies a living and holy sacrifice,
acceptable to God, which is your spiritual service of worship.
ROMANS 12:1 NASB

Simon and Andrew had no idea what was awaiting them that day when they hauled their nets out to the Sea of Galilee. Cast, pull, cast, pull. They wordlessly followed the routine they did every day, hauling in the fish that provided their livelihood as the hot breeze blew across their bare backs.

"Follow Me." Simon and Andrew looked at each other as those compelling words echoed through their minds. Although they may not have known Him personally, Jesus had been preaching repentance in the region of Galilee. His voice was authoritative, and they knew without a doubt they were being called. They immediately left their nets and followed Jesus.

Peter, initially listed with his birth name of Simon, was later the first disciple to be called "an apostle." He was bold and impetuous, often sticking his foot in his mouth. He was the only apostle to actually walk on water. He also was the one who rebuked Jesus when He talked of going to the cross. Peter was a real-life illustration of a sincere follower of Christ who, when tested, reverted to the flesh with disastrous results.

Matthew 16 tells the story. Jesus had just finished blessing Simon and given him the name "Peter" (from the Greek *petros,* or rock) in response to Peter's bold statement: "You are the Messiah, the Son of the living God!" (Matt. 16:16 NLT).

Then Jesus began to prepare His disciples for His final trip to Jerusalem. He told them that He was going to Jerusalem to die. "Peter took Him aside and began to rebuke Him, 'Oh no, Lord! This will never happen to you!' But He turned and told Peter, 'Get behind Me, Satan! You are an offense to Me because you are not thinking about God's concerns, but man's'" (Matt. 16:22–23).

What had happened? How could Peter announce, "You are the Messiah, the Son of the living God!" one moment and then immediately afterward miss what Jesus had been telling them all along? Jesus had come to die. He was ready to go to Jerusalem, where He must suffer, die and be buried, and rise again on the third day.

Peter could not comprehend Jesus's predictions! They simply weren't part of Peter's plan; they weren't what he wanted to happen to Jesus. Peter wanted Jesus to set up His kingdom there and then on the earth.

"Get behind Me, Satan!" Jesus chastised him. In other words, "You are being used as a pawn of the enemy, Peter." Consider this: If Peter, who actually walked with Jesus, could be used by the enemy, so can we. The enemy takes advantage when we walk in the flesh, when we want what we want and we don't look with Spirit eyes, seeing as God sees from His eternal vantage point.

We, too, can rebuke the Lord when we let our arrogance and pride take control.

Peter rebuked the Lord and was himself rebuked. He still had lessons to learn about living in the Spirit. He was desperately struggling to follow Christ in the strength of his flesh. He was living as a carnal Christian. He was about to take a crash course on the deceitfulness and weakness of his flesh.

Luke 22 paints the picture of Jesus's last hours. After three years of teaching His disciples about humility, on the night in which He was betrayed, He modeled humility for them. He had earlier wrapped a servant's towel around Himself and had washed the disciples' feet (see John 13:5). As they celebrated the Passover meal, He told them, "One of you will betray Me" (v. 21).

The men were confused and nearly speechless. They began to try to guess who the betrayer was, which led to an—can we just call it childish?—argument about which one of them was the greatest. Does it seem that they had missed everything Jesus had just told them?

The Lord turned to Peter. "Simon, Simon, behold, Satan has demanded permission to sift you like wheat; but I have prayed for you, that your faith may not fail; and you, when once you have turned again, strengthen your brothers" (Luke 22:31–32 NASB).

"Demanded"—*Webster's Collegiate Dictionary* offers these definitions of the verb: "to claim as due or just, to require." In other words, Satan had a claim on Peter. What was God allowing? He was allowing Peter to be sifted. The sifting would get rid of the old Simon Peter, the carnal Simon Peter, so that he could be Peter the *petros,* Peter the rock that Jesus had called him to be.

Sifting Reveals Fleshly Desires and Attitudes We Need to Cast Off

God does the same thing with us that He did with Peter. We are all going to go through trials that God allows, for in the midst of being tested and tried, the "yuck" in our lives comes to the surface. What a disgusting word, *yuck*. But it is an apt word for the aspects of our flesh that fight against the Spirit. When we are sifted, the yuck is separated out and exposed for what it is. We are then able to be cleansed of it so that we can clearly reflect the grace and the glory of God to a lost world. *Cleansing, refining, pruning, purifying, testing*—these are each words that describe the Holy Spirit's role in our lives.

The Bible paints yet another picture that helps us understand: God allows us to walk through valleys that are sometimes dark, desolate, and deserted. He does this so we can genuinely appreciate the breathtaking vistas at the mountaintops. It is in the valleys that we learn He will never leave us or forsake us and that He is just as faithful in the valleys as He is on the mountaintops. He is testing us, but He is always with us.

After Jesus told Peter that he would deny Him three times before the morning rooster crowed, Peter said to Jesus, in effect, "Whoa, Lord, I am ready to go to prison or even to be put to death for You! I am not going to deny you, not me!"

But Luke 22:54–62 (NASB) recounts what happened. Jesus had been arrested. They were leading Him away from the Garden of Gethsemane. Peter followed at a distance. A servant girl looked intently at him as he sat in the firelight and announced, "This man was with Him" (v. 56). But Peter denied it.

Soon a man insisted that he had seen Peter with Jesus: "You are one of them too!" (v. 58).

But Peter protested, "Man, I am not!" (v. 58).

About an hour passed and a third person must have heard the regional inflection in Peter's speech, because he began to insist that Peter was obviously a Galilean like Jesus and had been with Jesus too. Peter even more vehemently denied knowing Jesus: "Man, I do not know what you are talking about!" (v. 60). Matthew 26:74 even says that Peter peppered the denial with curses! Immediately a cock crowed, and "the Lord turned and looked at Peter" (Luke 22:61 NASB).

Can you *picture* such a look of grief, sorrow, and disappointment? Peter remembered the Lord's prediction and wept bitterly. Can you even imagine his despair as he saw Jesus being led away to be beaten, crucified, and buried?

We must stop here and ask ourselves if we, like Peter, are not setting ourselves up to deny Christ when we follow Him at a distance and warm ourselves at the world's fires.

John 21 tells the rest of the story. It is the account of Jesus's restoration of Peter—the *petros*. God's plan was for Peter to be a central foundation stone in the church that He was and is building. But He had to allow Peter to go through the refining process so that he could really be *petros*.

After the Crucifixion, Peter and some of the other disciples had retreated back to the Sea of Galilee, taking up their old trade of fishing. Peter must have felt hopeless and lost. I can imagine his thoughts: *Lord, there is no way You can use me again. I have committed the worst possible sin—I have denied You. How could You still love me?*

So Peter did what Peter knew how to do—he pushed his boat into the water and sat fishing all night long. Peter, Thomas, Nathanael, the two sons of Zebedee, and two others were with him—they must have been a glum group—and all were casting out but pulling in nothing. Jesus, whom they did not recognize at first, called to them from the seashore and advised them where to cast the net again for an abundance of fish. It was at that moment that Peter recognized the Lord. He jumped from the boat and made his way to the shore. After they had hauled in the net full of fish, Jesus offered them breakfast cooked over a fire He had made.

When they finished eating, Jesus asked Simon Peter, "Simon, son of John, do you love Me more than these?" (v. 15 NASB). The original Greek word for love in this verse is *agape,* which is God's unconditional love. He said, "Do you *agape* Me?"

Peter's answer was, "Yes, Lord; You know that I love You." The word "love" in this context was the Greek *phileo,* which means "brotherly love." I love You with a brotherly love. Do you see a difference in this Peter from the one who had boldly and brashly said, "I will go to prison and die for You"? In effect he was admitting, "Jesus, I love You with a brotherly love. I am not capable of *agape* love. I thought I was, but, Lord, I know myself better now. I am not capable of loving You like that, but I do love You; I love You with *phileo.*"

Jesus merely said, "Feed My lambs" (v. 15 HCSB). The Lord was commissioning Peter. He was calling him. He said to him a second time, "Simon, son of John, do you [*agape*] Me?"

Again Simon Peter answered, "Yes, Lord, . . . you know that I [*phileo*] You." This time Jesus said, "Shepherd My sheep" (v. 16).

Then Jesus asked the question in a slightly different way: "Simon, son of John, do you [*phileo*] Me?"

And Peter, grieved and exasperated, answered: "Lord, You know everything! You know that I [*phileo*] You."

And Jesus said simply to him, "Feed My sheep" (v. 17). Jesus called Peter three times—a parallel with Peter's three denials. But more importantly, in the third question Jesus met Peter where he was, at the point at which Peter was only capable of *phileo*. Jesus does the same for us. In love, He meets us where we are, at our point of human need and limitation, to take us where He wants us to be. When we warm ourselves at the Lord's fire, He will instruct us and commission us just as He did Peter.

It Is All About Love— God's First, Ours in Return

The Spirit-filled life is about each of us surrendering to what G. K. Chesterton called "the furious love of God." This surrender allows us to love Him in return, because if we love Him, we will not fear but will trust Him. Scripture tells us, "There is no fear in love; instead, perfect love drives out fear" (1 John 4:18). Once we realize His love is perfect, we will not have any problem entrusting ourselves totally and completely to Him, crucifying any of the flesh that is left and coming to Him willingly. We'll be able to accomplish what Paul urges us to do in Romans 12:1: "Therefore, brothers, by the mercies of God, I urge you to present your bodies as a living sacrifice, holy and pleasing to God; this is your spiritual worship."

It is an act of worship to offer ourselves to the Lord. That is what happened to Peter. He realized who and what he was and that the resources of his flesh were not enough to live the Christian life. That is exactly where God wants all of us to be— at the end of ourselves, empty, so the Holy Spirit can fill us and empower us just as He did Peter on the day of Pentecost.

Just ten days after Jesus's ascension to heaven, God poured out the Holy Spirit on His believers, an event recorded in Acts 2. Some in the crowd thought the believers were drunk, but Peter stood in front of thousands of people and explained, "No, we are not drunk. It is just nine o'clock in the morning. What you don't understand is that the Spirit of God has been sent upon us. This is the Holy Spirit that has filled us" (see Acts 2:14–18).

Peter began to present the gospel to them in such a compelling way that he was even able to say, "It is this Jesus, whom you crucified" (see v. 22). What boldness—but boldness redeemed for God's glory this time.

God did not wipe out Peter's personality—rather, He redeemed it. Peter's boldness and impulsiveness that had brought grief and near destruction to his own life was now channeled and empowered by the Holy Spirit of God. God then used that very bold Peter to step forward on the day of Pentecost. More than three thousand people were saved.

Note, however, that God did not entrust that responsibility to Peter until Peter came to the end of himself. Similarly, God will not entrust an outpouring of His Spirit and the riches of His secrets to people who are not willing to trust only Him. We cannot continue to live life in the flesh and expect to know the secret things of God. We cannot expect to know things that other people don't know if we are still trying to decipher them through the flesh. We must be willing to nail our fleshly desires to the cross daily and follow Christ. That's every day. Every day we must die to self. Every time a circumstance arises that tests our patience or anger we have to say, "Lord, I give it to You. Father, I release this. Lord, meet me, fill me, respond through me in the midst of this as only You can do. Father, I need Your patience, Your love," or whatever the need may be.

After Peter finally let go of Peter, God used him in ways that he probably never would have imagined. Peter became a leader of the early church. And Peter, not a learned scholar or a rabbi, was entrusted by God to write two books of the New Testament! Peter's life offers a promise for us that no matter what has happened in our past, when we give ourselves to Jesus Christ, He will empower us and use us for His glory. He will always go far above and beyond anything we could begin to ask or imagine. It was Peter himself who said, "And the God of all grace, who called you to his eternal glory in Christ, after you have suffered a little while, will himself *restore* you and make you *strong, firm* and *steadfast*" (1 Pet. 5:10 NIV, emphasis mine). We know that twice Jesus had told Peter that he would die a death like Jesus's own, and tradition records that Peter was in fact, crucified. However, not feeling worthy to be crucified like his Lord, he was crucified upside down.

First Peter 1:3–9 reveals the new Peter:

Blessed be the God and Father of our Lord Jesus Christ. According to His great mercy, He has given us a new birth into a living hope through the resurrection of Jesus Christ from the dead, and into an inheritance that is imperishable, uncorrupted, and unfading, kept in heaven for you, who are being protected by God's power through faith for a salvation that is ready to be revealed in the last time. You rejoice in this, though now for a short time you have had to be distressed by various trials so that the genuineness of your faith—more valuable than gold, which perishes though refined by fire—may result in praise, glory, and honor at the revelation of Jesus Christ. You love Him, though you have not seen Him. And though not seeing Him now, you believe in Him and rejoice with inexpressible and glorious joy, because you are receiving the goal of your faith, the salvation of your souls.

The Peter who previously did not want to suffer is now saying we will be perfected through suffering. He is telling believers to be glad. There is wonderful joy ahead even though it is necessary to endure many trials for a while. These trials are only to test our faith and to show that it is strong and pure. It is being tested as fire tests and purifies gold, and our faith is far more precious to God than mere gold. Then if our faith remains strong after being tried by fiery trials, it will bring us much praise and glory and honor on the day when Jesus Christ is revealed to the whole world.

God's Promises Await Us at the End of Ourselves

If you are not gloriously joyful in your walk with the Lord, ask yourself whether you believe God's promises. Unbelief is the source of a life lived according to the flesh. Like Peter, we must come to the end of ourselves today and say, "Lord, I believe."

When Jesus came down from the Mount of Transfiguration, He healed a demonized boy. The Lord said to the boy's father, "If you can believe, all things are possible" (Mark 9:23 NKJV), and the young father cried out, "Lord, I believe; Help my unbelief!" (v. 24).

We can also ask God to help us believe: "Father, I want to believe with every fiber of my being. Help me, help me. Rid me of unbelief." If we let go, we will experience the promises and the spiritual growth that Peter describes in 2 Peter 1:3–8, and we'll find ourselves doing what Peter instructs us to do at the end of the passage:

> For His divine power has given us everything required for life and godliness, through the knowledge of Him who called us by His own glory and goodness. By these He has given us very great and precious promises, so that through them you may share in the divine nature, escaping the corruption that is in the world because of evil desires. For this very reason, make every effort to supplement your faith with goodness, goodness with knowledge, knowledge with self-control, self-control with endurance, endurance with godliness, godliness with brotherly affection, and brotherly affection with love. For if these qualities are yours and are increasing, they will keep you from being useless or unfruitful in the knowledge of our Lord Jesus Christ.

What an awesome promise! We will share in God's divine nature—and this is only one of the promises God makes. Learning what God's promises are is the foundation for spiritual growth. That is one of the reasons for Bible study. When we learn what God's promises are, we can begin to apply them to our lives. Did you notice the spiritual progression in the above passage? Your faith will produce a life of moral excellence. Such a life leads to knowing God better, because if we have His commands and we obey them, He reveals Himself to us. Knowing God leads to self-control. Self-control leads to patient endurance, and patient endurance leads to godliness. Godliness leads to affection for other Christians, and that affection leads into love for the people in our wider world. This progression is the path to maturity in Christ. Jesus said, "By this all people will know that you are My disciples, if you have love for one another" (John 13:35).

The mark of spiritual maturity is love. It is love for God. It is love for other Christians. Ultimately, it is love for everyone. When we see and accept ourselves for who we really are, we then turn ourselves over to the Lord and we allow Him to empower us, fill us, and live through us. He gives us Spirit eyes that see as He sees. We begin to see below the surface level: we see the hearts and the lives of struggling, hurting Christians around us. We find that instead of criticizing them, we come alongside them as brothers or sisters in faith, praying for and walking with them until they're ready to walk again on their own.

We will also look out at a lost world, and our hearts will be grieved. We will sense the compassion of our Lord because we are so full of His Spirit that He will begin to manifest His heart and His mind in our lives. And as part of that divine nature, we will have deep compassion for a lost world. Suddenly the things that so easily entangled us in the past no longer will entangle us. They won't even entice us. We will care less and less for the things of this world. We will care only about that better country, the one we have set our eyes on, the one we can hardly wait to be a part of. A. W. Tozer wrote about the inward ability to behold God in *The Pursuit of God.* He said, "A new set of eyes (so to speak) will develop within us enabling us to be looking at God while our outward eyes are seeing the scenes of this passing world" (89–90). While still in this world, we will desire to be used to bring Him glory and to advance the kingdom of God.

By this point it should be apparent that we need to love God. How? By surrendering to His immeasurable love for us. "Surrender" is perhaps as unpopular a term now as it's ever been, and yet there is no other way to experience God's love. To *live* life from the inside out, we must *be changed* from the inside out. We are to love Him with complete and utter abandon and to love others the same way. When we come to the end of ourselves, we will experience His perfect love.

God's greatest commandment, Jesus reminded us, is this: "Love the Lord your God with all your heart, with all your soul, and with all your mind. . . . The second is like it: Love your neighbor as yourself" (Matt. 22:37, 39).

The only way we can love God and others is to walk in the Spirit, living life as mature Christians. Mary chose that life, and Jesus said, "Mary has chosen the good part, which shall not be taken away from her" (Luke 10:42 NASB). Choose love. Utterly abandon yourself to the furious love of our God, who is pursuing you. He wants you to come to that place at the end of yourself where He takes over. It is then that He does what only He can do. He fills you with joy inexpressible, and others will be drawn to Him as they see His love in your life. It is all about love.

6

How about a Love Checkup?

*If I speak the languages of men
and of angels, but do not have love,
I am a sounding gong or a clanging cymbal.*

1 CORINTHIANS 13:1

*A*my Carmichael was an unlikely missionary candidate. An Irish girl born in 1867, she grew up in a country of long, dreary, rainy winters that must have made her unrelenting pain even worse. Amy suffered from neuralgia—a chronic, painful disease of the nerves. This condition left Amy bedridden for weeks on end. When Hudson Taylor, a missionary, came to her community in 1887, she went to hear him. Hudson wasn't the only one she heard—God called her to India, as extreme in its steamy heat as Ireland was in its damp and cold. There, in spite of her debilitating disease, she found her lifelong vocation. She rescued many babies and young girls from a life destined for forced prostitution in Hindu temples. Amy was beloved by all who knew her and especially by the nearly one thousand children at the sanctuary she founded for them in Dohnavur.

This incredible woman of God wrote a little book entitled *If.* In it Amy explains the source of her thoughts on "Calvary Love" that make up this small volume: "One evening a fellow-worker brought me a problem about a younger one who was missing the way of Love. This led to a wakeful night, for the word at such times is always, 'Lord, is it I? Have I failed her anywhere? What do I know of Calvary love?' And then sentence by sentence the 'Ifs' came, almost as if spoken aloud in the inward ear" (5).

Here is a sample of what Amy wrote that night. "If I refuse to be a corn of wheat that falls into the ground and dies ('is separated from all in which it lived before'), then I know nothing of Calvary love" (74). To say it a bit differently, I won't know what Christ's love is if I am not willing to die to myself, to deny myself, and to take up my cross daily and follow Him.

Being in Denial Is a Good Thing When It Refers to Denial of Self

Do we understand that the God of the universe put on skin, became one of us, and willingly lived in this sin-sick world but was yet untainted by sin? He walked perfectly before men and the Father and then willingly laid down His life. His blood poured out on the ground for us. If He can love us that much, can we not trust Him with our lives, with everything we have, with everything He has entrusted to us? Can we not offer it back to Him by dying to ourselves and choosing only to live for Him? If we are going to walk in freedom, in the fullness of His Spirit, we must come to the end of ourselves. It is the Spirit-filled life that leads to More.

Our flesh will scream for recognition at times, trying to convince us to settle for less. Though our emotions may demand loudly for us to listen to them, that "still small voice" will be easier to hear as we daily give up our will and are absorbed into His. When someone close to us does something hurtful, the Spirit will remind us that love doesn't take into account a wrong suffered. Love doesn't keep a list of offenses. Love is patient. Love is kind. It is that voice that draws us to Him. It is the lovingkindness of God that draws us to repentance and gives us the desire to spend time with Him and to want to be like Him.

How does the love of God fit into a life that is broken yet whole again, dead and yet more alive than ever in Jesus Christ? How is God's love fleshed out in my daily actions? Amy Carmichael described it this way: "If a sudden jar can cause me to speak an impatient unloving word, then I know nothing of Calvary love. For a cup brim full of sweet water cannot spill even one drop of bitter water however suddenly jolted" (46). In other words, if someone is unexpectedly rude to me and that unexpected arrow seemingly out of nowhere can cause me to speak an impatient or unloving word, do I really understand Calvary love? If my heart is full of Christ, what will come out of my mouth when I am bumped or jostled? When verbal attacks wound me or someone hurts my feelings, what should people see in my response? *Who* should they see? They should see Christ, manifested in compassion and forgiveness. Do they see Him? If the Word of God has come in and has separated the soul from the spirit, if it has exposed those things in me that need to be taken off, then there should not be any of the flesh left to come out when I am squeezed. Instead, the Spirit-man should rise to the surface and spill out for all to see.

Jesus often used images from farming, maybe because so many of His followers could immediately identify with it. Luke 6:43–45 records another of Jesus's comparisons: "For a good tree does not bear bad fruit, nor does a bad tree bear good fruit. For every tree is known by its own fruit. For men do not gather figs from thorns, nor do they gather grapes from a bramble bush. A good man out of the good treasure of his heart brings forth good; and an evil man out of the evil treasure of his heart brings forth evil. For out of the abundance of the heart his mouth speaks" (NKJV).

Jesus also gave us the law of love: "You have heard that it was said, Love your neighbor and hate your enemy. But I tell you, love your enemies and pray for those who persecute you, so that you may be sons of your Father in heaven. For He causes His sun to rise on the evil and the good, and sends rain on the righteous and the unrighteous. For if you love those who love you, what reward will you have? Don't even the tax collectors do the same? And if you greet only your brothers, what are you doing out of the ordinary? Don't even the Gentiles do the same? Be perfect, therefore, as your heavenly Father is perfect" (Matt. 5:43–48).

God has set the standard of love. As His children, we are called to live life on a higher plain, no longer as mere ordinary people. We are called to so much More.

Years ago, my son Grant sometimes played with a boy in our neighborhood. The boy had a habit of picking on Grant. This boy's birthday was approaching, and he talked openly about the party he was planning. Every afternoon Grant got off the bus, and as soon as he came in the door, he asked, "Did my invitation come in the mail?" Each time I had to tell him no. My heart broke for him. Party day came and went. We planned something else to do so Grant wouldn't be home while everyone else was celebrating at the party.

I have to admit: I kicked into the mother-bear-protecting-her-cubs mode. The next time I saw that little boy I nearly growled! I knew then that it was time for prayer.

"Father, You know I am having a hard time with this." In response, God impressed upon me this conviction: *Pray for his mother, Donna. Pray for him. Pray for them.* I began to intercede for that family, and slowly my attitude changed.

A couple of years passed and a crisis hit the family. The boy's mother called me, and by that time there was only love in my heart for her. I shared with her that I had been praying for her and for her family. God used me to help her walk through that difficult time in her life, yet I would have been totally unprepared had I not listened to the voice of the Holy Spirit.

At the time I witnessed the injustice done to Grant, everything in me was saying "protect your child." The truth is, I protect my child best by being right with the Lord—by not allowing sin in my life. Love is being willing to love those who hurt us. It is being willing to pray for those who persecute us or our children or our grandchildren. It is knowing that in the midst of any situation, God will work through it for good.

Giving Ourselves a Regular Love Checkup Is Essential

If love is so important—and we know it is—we should evaluate how we're doing keeping love always as our goal. First Corinthians 13:4–8 gives us guidelines, but we need to make them practical and specific. How do I treat my spouse, my children, my friends, my acquaintances, and even more importantly, those who seem to have a grudge against me? Is love my response to them? My friend Sylvia Gunter, in her book *Prayer Portions,* suggests using 1 Corinthians 13 as a "love checkup." I have taken her suggestion and adapted it for our purposes. Read the following and evaluate your own performance.

1. *Love is patient.* Would my children, spouse, or friend say I am patient? Do I listen to them without checking my watch as they are sharing the concerns of their day with me?

2. *Love is kind.* Am I kind to everyone, not just those who are kind to me? Do I encourage the inexperienced checkout clerk?

3. *Love does not envy.* Am I happy without jealousy at others' blessings? Do I applaud them with sincere good wishes when they receive something that I wish I had or when their spouse gets a huge raise at work?

4. *Love is not boastful.* Do I keep the glowing, prideful reports about my children to myself, rejoicing in the accomplishments of other people's children?

5. *Love is not conceited and does not act improperly.* Do I ask God to forgive me for feeling superior to those who don't seem to make the "wise choices" about life that I've made? Do I keep myself from gossiping and otherwise acting in ways that tarnish my Christian reputation?

6. *Love is not selfish.* Do I push and jostle to be first in line at the cash register? Do I always have to have my way?

7. *Love is not provoked.* Do I boil over at the small things that my spouse, child, parent, employer, or another person does that seem designed just to irritate me?
8. *Love does not keep a record of wrongs.* Do I hold grudges over thoughtless comments or deeds by other people? Do I keep a mental tally of times I've been left out or slighted?

Again I am reminded of the words of Amy Carmichael: "If I dredge up a confessed, repented, and forsaken sin against another and allow my remembrance of sin to color my thinking and feed my suspicions, then I know nothing of Calvary love" (28).

Calvary love is forgiveness. Calvary love is the father of the prodigal, hoping the best, thinking the best, waiting for the slightest response that his loved one wants to come back to the Lord. It's being there to embrace that person, to walk with him or her, to say, "I knew it was within you. I knew you would come back to the Lord." Love encourages them to come back to His open arms.

There are additional aspects of love to evaluate, asking ourselves how they apply to our daily walk. Love is never glad about injustice. Love rejoices when truth wins out. Love absolutely never gives up. Love never loses faith. Love looks into the eyes and into the heart of others and sees the best. Love sees beyond what a person was in the past and where they came from. Love chooses to see whom God has created and purposed for that person to become for His glory.

The words of 1 Corinthians 13:7 remind us: Love "bears all things, believes all things, hopes all things, endures all things."

What peaceful, nonconfrontational, stalwart, and steadfast words are these: *bearing, believing, hoping, enduring.* None of these responses to life's arrows and darts are possible without our coming to the end of ourselves and allowing the Spirit to show His perfect love through us. Dying to self will lead to that perfect peace that only the Lord can provide. It's the peace that our loving Father will give to us as we practice the love that is both a commandment and a gift.

7

Where the Battle
Is Won

The LORD is my light and my salvation—
whom should I fear?
The LORD is the stronghold of my life—
of whom should I be afraid?

PSALM 27:1

If you read the newspaper or watch any news coverage on TV, you may have come across the word *stronghold.* Makeshift strongholds occupied by insurgents in battle zones provide a place from which snipers can shoot or from which explosives can be set off by remote control. According to *Webster's Collegiate Dictionary,* the literal meaning of *stronghold* is "a fortified place, a place of security or survival." There were many strongholds erected in biblical times—Masada, high above the Dead Sea region, is one of the most famous. I have been to this flat-topped mountain that rises thirteen hundred feet above sea level and faces the western shore of the Dead Sea. It was the desert fortress of Herod the Great. Masada was built as a safe place in case of insurrection or attack.

Often Bible heroes took refuge in strongholds both to spy on and hide from their enemies.

A stronghold can also be a place of refuge for the soul. In 2 Samuel 22:2–3, David, after being delivered from Saul, sang a song of praise to the Lord that went like this: "The LORD is my rock, my fortress and my deliverer; my God is my rock, in whom I take refuge, my shield and the horn of my salvation. He is my stronghold, my refuge and my savior—from violent men you save me" (NIV).

In *The Weathering Grace of God,* Ken Gire says, "Our intimacy with the Lord is our Masada. That is our place of refuge. That is our source of strength. That is our very present help in time of trouble. Masadas are not built in times of trouble. They are peace-time projects, built and fortified in times of stability. If we wait until the upheaval to begin building, there won't be a fortress to run to" (60).

Strongholds Can Become Places of Fear Rather Than Refuge

All of us long for a safe place. Sadly, many times we utilize the world's strongholds or the ones provided by our enemy. Like Adam and Eve, we hide. When we do, we are running from the only One who is our sure refuge.

Our strongholds are cheap replicas of the real thing. They are places of fear we cling to and hide within, thinking falsely that we will be protected. Any stronghold we construct becomes a trap. As my friend Joni Shankles says, "The protection we can create looks big and strong. But any protection built in our own strength is really only an open door to the enemy. Satan has the master key to come uninvited and unstoppable through any walls built with the resources of the flesh."

We must dismantle these strongholds of our own creation stone by stone. We must remind ourselves that we were originally designed to live life from the inside out. But our fallen nature cautions us to live life from the outside in, shutting ourselves in our makeshift fortresses. We must ask the Holy Spirit to help us knock down those strongholds and fill us so we can live life the way God intended it to be lived.

See if you recognize any of the building materials for these strongholds:

- *Rejection.* When you walk into a room filled with women you don't yet know, what do you find yourself thinking? Do you ever wonder, *Do I fit in? Am I dressed nicely enough? Do they like me? Are they going to ask me to lunch?* And if you're one of the group who already knows each other, what do you find yourself thinking? *She's probably too busy. She won't want to go to lunch with us. She probably wouldn't want to spend time with us*—and yet you haven't asked her if she'd like to come. It's part of our human nature not to want to feel rejected. But feeling accepted starts with us, not with the other person. If we take the focus off ourselves and look at those around us, we will be more perceptive and willing to step outside our comfort zones and draw someone in. We'll want to make sure they feel comfortable, significant, and know that the Lord loves them.

- *Woundedness and pain.* We are often afraid of being hurt. Because of that, many times we only allow people to get "so close." Afraid to take a risk, we miss out on the opportunities God gives us to show that we are His disciples by loving others like that "friend who stays closer than a brother" (Prov. 18:24).

- *Exposure.* We're afraid that if people really know us, if they know who and what we really are inside, they will reject us. We are afraid they won't love us. The truth is that none of us is completely lovable inside. Yet Jesus accepts all of us unconditionally and draws us to Himself. He takes us from where we are to where we need to be, just as He did with Peter. Confident of His unconditional love, we will be willing to risk being known.

God wants us to lay all of those old feelings aside. We must dismantle the walls of our self-protection and allow the Spirit of God to come in and build a protective stronghold around us, a stronghold constructed of love, healing, and wholeness.

So how do we tear down the strongholds the enemy erects in our life?

We Must Take to Heart the Truth That God Is Our Only Worthy Stronghold

In Psalm 18, David sings about the source of our strength in words very similar to those we read in 2 Samuel: "I love You, Lord, my strength. The Lord is my rock, my fortress, and my deliverer, my God, my mountain where I seek refuge, my shield and the horn of my salvation, my stronghold. I called to the Lord, who is worthy of praise, and I was saved from my enemies" (vv. 2–3).

It is the Lord who protects us from the schemes of our enemies. He is our safe place! He is our stronghold. He is not a stone but a rock. The Lord is the very bedrock of our spiritual security. He is the One we praise.

David certainly recognized the safety found in God. His words echo in the psalms:

- "The LORD is my light and my salvation—whom should I fear? The LORD is the stronghold of my life—of whom should I be afraid?" (Ps. 27:1).
- "Incline Your ear to me, rescue me quickly; Be to me a rock of strength, A stronghold to save me" (Ps. 31:2 NASB).
- "He alone is my rock and my salvation, my stronghold; I will never be shaken" (Ps. 62:2).

An old hymn says, "On Christ the solid Rock I stand." Standing on this sure foundation is one of the keys to More. When Christ is our foundation, we will not be easily shaken. But why aren't we standing on Him? Often it's because we're depending on ourselves.

Zechariah 2:5 lays down the Lord's words on behalf of the city of Jerusalem: "I will be a wall of fire around it, and I will be the glory within it." That image applies mightily to our twenty-first-century spiritual lives. Have you watched coverage of forest or brush fires on television and seen the way the fire can become a massive, threatening, impenetrable wall, unapproachable from the outside, locking everything inside it? Think of that wall of fire as another kind of stronghold. That's the kind of protection we can expect from God, and when we're on the inside of it, we're protected from the evil one. God says, I want to be your safe place. If you depend upon Me, you won't be easily shaken. You are not going down. You *will* stand firm.

Second Kings 6:1–23 describes a wall of fire around Elisha and how the Lord opened the eyes of Elisha's servant so that he could see what was taking place in the spirit realm. The king of Aram and his army were waging war against Israel. The Holy Spirit told Elisha where the king of Aram and his army were camping, and Elisha warned the king of Israel.

Every time the king of Aram would try to set a trap for the Israelites, Elisha warned the king of Israel. Angry at being thwarted in his battle plans, the king of Aram said to one of his servants, "Tell me, which one of us is for the king of Israel?" (v. 11). In other words, there must be a spy in the camp. Who is it?

The servant set the king straight about what was going on. "No one, my lord the king. Elisha, the prophet in Israel, tells the king of Israel even the words you speak in your bedroom" (v. 12)— in other words, the strategic military secrets that the king of Aram assumed no one but his inner circle would know.

The king of Aram was determined to capture Elisha. He found out where he would be staying and sent a massive army to capture him, surrounding the city under cover of darkness.

Can you imagine walking outside in the morning to find an entire army ringed around your home? That's what happened to Elisha's servant. He reported to Elisha, asking, "Oh, my master, what are we to do?" (v. 15).

Was Elisha fearful? Not at all. He answered the servant, "Don't be afraid, for those who are with us outnumber those who are with them" (v. 16).

Elisha prayed, "Lord, please open his eyes and let him see." Second Kings 6:17 describes what happened: "So the Lord opened the servant's eyes. He looked and saw that the mountain was covered with horses and chariots of fire all around Elisha."

Here's the rest of the story: Elisha prayed that the king of Aram's army would be struck blind. Then Elisha led the blinded army all the way down to Samaria and presented them to the king of Israel. The king, relying on Elisha's godly counsel, asked Elisha whether he should kill these prisoners of war.

"Don't kill them," Elisha advised. "Set food and water in front of them so they can eat and drink and go to their master."

The king took Elisha's advice, preparing a feast for them; and when they had eaten he let them go, with their sight restored, sending them back to the king of Aram. That was the last the Israelites saw of those raiders!

There is a very real unseen world. When we make the Lord our stronghold, He will put that wall of fire around us. He will protect us with His angels and their chariots of fire if we will trust in Him. He also provides the spiritual weaponry for us to fight the enemy, who is most decidedly a spiritual one. Second Corinthians 10:3–5 explains, "For although we are walking in the flesh, we do not wage war in a fleshly way, since the weapons of our warfare are not fleshly, but are powerful through God for the demolition of strongholds. We demolish arguments and every high-minded thing that is raised up against the knowledge of God, taking every thought captive to the obedience of Christ."

By "every high-minded thing" Paul means every imagination, every idea, and every thought that has tried to elevate itself above the truth of God's Word. We are exposing them and we are pulling down these counterfeit strongholds, what Francis Frangipane, in *The Three Battlegrounds,* calls a "house made of thoughts." He further explains, "It is important to recognize that, in speaking of strongholds (2 Corinthians 10:1–5) the apostle is addressing *the church!* It is foolish to assume that our salvation experience has eliminated all the wrong ideas and attitudes—the strongholds—which are still influencing our perceptions and behaviors" (31).

Out with the Counterfeit, In with the Real

But how do we manage to dismantle these counterfeit strongholds? We do not do it by our will, by gritting our teeth, or by trying harder. There is a wonderful heavenly paradox in how we tear down those false refuges. We do it through *not* doing those things. We demolish false strongholds through surrender and dependence on God's power. We say to the Lord, "In the power of Jesus Christ and His shed blood, I am taking authority over these wrong ways of thinking. They are coming down; they will not be left standing!" Like a building about to be demolished, these false habits of thinking are about to be history.

A planned building implosion is an awe-inspiring event to watch. Recently a company in charge of a demolition project prepared to level the building by boring fourteen hundred holes in the concrete columns that made up the supports for the building. The holes weakened the support structure in preparation for the next step, the strategic placement of dynamite throughout the building. With its support structure already compromised, once the explosives were ignited, the building fell in on itself.

Similarly, the Sword of the Spirit, which is the truth of God's Word, bores holes in those strongholds of lies that have been erected in our minds. As we get to know and take to heart God's Word it weakens the fleshly and Satanic thoughts that bolster our little counterfeit places of refuge. When we come against those strongholds and we poke their shabby foundations with the Sword of the Spirit, we are weakening them thrust by thrust. Through the power of prayer and the blood of Jesus Christ, we are taking authority over them and demolishing them.

Once they're gone, there's still one thing left to do, and it is essential. We ourselves must clear off the debris. This does take some action on our part because it's an act of the will. We must haul off every fragment of the old nature so that we with the help of the Holy Spirit can build in its place a refuge of truth based on God's Word.

We want to rebuild on the foundation of Christ. We build these strongholds using God's Word. By faith we replace the wrong ways of thinking with God's truth. As we meditate on His Word day and night, His Word becomes a part of who we are. God's Word inevitably changes our actions because our actions originate as thoughts.

8
Off with the Old!

You're done with that old life. It's like a filthy set of ill-fitting
clothes you've stripped off and put in the fire.
COLOSSIANS 3:10a (MSG)

*T*he layered look is in again this year," announced some fashion magazines recently, as they do from time to time. The layered approach works especially well when you're a tourist in a climate that has a wide variation in temperatures throughout the day or that is unpredictable from hour to hour. It also works in West Tennessee, where I live. Tennesseans have a saying: "If you don't like the weather, wait a few minutes." From a practical standpoint, if you wear two or three light layers instead of one heavy one, not only will you be warmer when it's cold because the air between the layers acts as insulation, but you can just simply peel off the top layer or layers as the temperatures rise. It's easy to do, right? At least with clothing.

It's not so easy when we have to peel away our old nature, but it's a requirement if we want to experience the More that is promised to us by our Father.

One layer that must be ruthlessly discarded is our self-concern. When we become focused on ourselves, we can become paranoid, finding ourselves developing false assumptions about other people, not to mention about ourselves. We must stop focusing on self and set our minds on things above, on those things that really matter. Here's a news flash: It is not about us. It is all about Jesus. "For to me, to live is Christ and to die is gain," Paul said (Phil. 1:21 NASB).

I reminded myself of that verse when each of my three daughters was in the fourth grade. The reason for that reminder was the annual fourth-grade trip to Camp Cosby, a YMCA camp deep in the backwoods of Alabama. This rustic, and I do mean rustic, camp is designed to allow suburban children to experience nature firsthand with such events as wolf spider hunting (at night by flashlight), canoeing, and hiking wooded trails day and night without the comforts and conveniences of city life. It's never been something I looked forward to, though, and I've had to pray, "Lord, redeem this time for You. Put me in a cabin with a little girl who needs somebody who will love her and give her attention. I'll put my desire for a soft, warm bed in my own home aside for the opportunity that I pray You'll bring my way."

On these three different occasions, I chose a good attitude and headed off for the mandatory wilderness experience. The camp experience I looked forward to the most each year was rising early in the morning while the sky was still dark and the camp was quiet and heading down to the lake with my Bible and flashlight. The year I went to camp with my middle daughter, Alli, I experienced one of those ethereal moments. I had been reading in Psalms, and I leaned back to look up at the brilliant starlit sky. I was marveling at God's handiwork. "Truly the heavens declare the glory of God" (Ps. 19:1). Suddenly I saw not one shooting star but two shoot across the sky. In the theater of His creation, for an audience of one, God sent a grand display of His artistic handiwork. I squealed with delight and felt as though the Father was saying, "I see you and I love you!"

I practically floated back to the cabin, and a little girl who I had earlier noticed watching me closely, asked, "So, where is it that you go every morning?"

I answered, "I take my Bible with me, and I go down by the lake. It is beautiful down there. This morning I read some Scripture and prayed and I spent some quiet time in the presence of the Lord because He loves me and He loves you. He's my heavenly Father." What a privilege to be able to share that joy with a little girl! These opportunities will come to you when you shed that old comfort-seeking, security-demanding self.

Cast Off Your Old Sinful Nature As You Would a Dress That No Longer Fits

Ephesians 4:17–32, the New Living Translation (NLT), picks up the idea of shedding layers of clothing. The layered look might be attractive in fashion but not in our inner person. We are to peel those things off that we have been depending upon. Paul tells us what to do (the italics are mine):

> With the Lord's authority I say this: Live no longer as the Gentiles do, for they are hopelessly confused. Their minds are full of darkness; they wander far from the life God gives because they have closed their minds and hardened their hearts against him. They have no

sense of shame. They live for lustful pleasure and eagerly practice every kind of impurity.

But that isn't what you learned about Christ. Since you have heard about Jesus and have learned the truth that comes from him, *throw off* your old sinful nature and your former way of life, which is corrupted by lust and deception. Instead, let the Spirit renew your thoughts and attitudes. *Put on* your new nature, created to be like God—truly righteous and holy.

So stop telling lies. Let us tell our neighbors the truth, for we are all parts of the same body. And "don't sin by letting anger control you." Don't let the sun go down while you are still angry, for anger gives a foothold to the devil.

If you are a thief, quit stealing. Instead, use your hands for good hard work, and then give generously to others in need. Don't use foul or abusive language. Let everything you say be good and helpful, so that your words will be an encouragement to those who hear them.

And do not bring sorrow to God's Holy Spirit by the way you live. Remember, he has identified you as his own, guaranteeing that you will be saved on the day of redemption.

Get rid of all bitterness, rage, anger, harsh words, and slander, as well as all types of evil behavior. Instead, be kind to each other, tenderhearted, forgiving one another, just as God through Christ has forgiven you.

At the beginning of the section above, Paul draws a contrast between those who have heard about Jesus and learned the truth and those who are still lost and confused, wandering around in the filthy rags of sin, shame, and impurity. He declares in Romans 1:28 about those who continue in sin: "God gave them over to a depraved mind" (NASB). They were filled with such nasty attitudes as unrighteousness, wickedness, greed, evil, envy, murder, strife, deceit, and malice (see v. 29). He goes on to explain that these people will be gossipers, slanderers, haters of God, insolent, arrogant, boastful, inventors of evil, disobedient to parents, without understanding, untrustworthy, unloving, and unmerciful (see vv. 29–31). And these attitudes and behaviors lead ultimately to willful disregard for God's laws: "Although they know the ordinance of God, that those who practice such things are worthy of death, they not only do the same, but also give hearty approval to those who practice them" (v. 32 NASB).

What an ironic reversal of what God offers us! There is never enough to satisfy once you get in that mode. "There's Gotta Be More" turns into a mockery as the thirst for evil becomes insatiable. Like us, the nonbelieving world knows there must be more. We can all be guilty of trying to meet this craving in illegitimate ways. And when we do, those ways then take control.

So Paul tells us we are to take off that old way of life. In the NLT's modern terms, just what does that mean? In a matter-of-fact way Paul lists many of the attitudes that we are to shed:

1. We are to take off lust and deception. That means we are not to act impulsively on the desires of our bodies and we are not to allow ourselves to be deluded or to cheat or delude others.

2. We are to take off falsehood, to stop telling lies. That means we are to walk in the truth, and the only way to do that is to know the Word of God. Why is it so easy to lie? For one thing, it is a part of our sin nature. It also goes back to that whole need to protect ourselves. We are so afraid of rejection. We tell ourselves that if we are totally honest about who we are—if we don't make ourselves look better than we really are or make the situation look better than it really is—then we are not going to be accepted. We must refuse to live like this because when we move into that false place, we open the door to the enemy once again. We must speak, live, and walk in truth.

3. We are to take off stealing. Don't take what isn't yours. That doesn't just mean money, something many of us would never dream of taking. It also means we are not to steal someone else's reputation, someone else's happiness or peace, or somebody's spouse. We are not to steal. We are not to take what doesn't belong to us.

4. We are to take off foul or abusive language. These words translated literally from the Greek mean "rotten worthless words that are bad and corrupt." In Matthew 12:34–37, Jesus issues a strong warning about words: "Brood of vipers! How can you speak good things when you are evil? For the mouth speaks from the overflow of the heart. A good man produces good things from his storeroom of good, and an evil man produces evil things from his storeroom of evil. I tell you that on the day of judgment people will have to account for every careless word they speak. For by your words you will be acquitted, and by your words you will be condemned."

Jesus was speaking to men—but these words seem so "made for a woman." Many of us would probably rank high on a verbal skills continuum. Jesus says we are going to be held accountable for what we say. If that doesn't make us stop and think before we speak, I don't know what will.

All of our children, our son included, have been highly verbal. Sometimes I've found myself wishing for just five minutes of peace. Our youngest daughter is probably the most talkative of the four. She'll wander around the house following me like a shadow, asking me seemingly endless questions and chattering about anything and everything. Really, it's charming in a child— but occasionally I feel that I've been bombarded with words.

How many times are we guilty of saying too much or of saying lots of words but with little wisdom? We must guard our mouths because Scripture says we will be judged by what we speak. "The mouth speaks from the overflow of the heart," Jesus warns. If love for Jesus Christ fills us, what we say will please Him and bring honor to Him. Our heart's desire will be to make Jesus known, to let others know how much they are loved, and to help them understand how precious and beautiful they are in His sight.

5. *We are to take off bitterness.* The root, or maybe the twin, of bitterness is unforgiveness. *Webster's* defines *bitter* as "acrid, astringent, or disagreeable; distasteful or distressing to the mind; accompanied by severe pain or suffering; marked by cynicism; intensely unpleasant"—and that's just a partial definition.

The word *acrid* sheds further light on the nuances of *bitter.* Acrid means "sharp and harsh or unpleasantly pungent in taste or odor." In other words, it stinks. It tastes bad. It smells bad. It's a poison that's irritating and corrosive. My husband, Steve, made this comment: "Bitterness and unforgiveness are acids that eat through their containers."

Paul warns us in Hebrews 12:15: "See to it that no one falls short of the grace of God and that no root of bitterness springs up, causing trouble and by it, defiling many." Bitterness poisons us, sometimes even physically. It is like a cancer. It eats away at us and then it poisons other people, too, seeping out of us and doing its damage to every person who crosses our path.

6. We are to take off any angry attitudes that are in danger of controlling us. In Greek, the word for anger is *orgia,* from which we get *orgy,* which we think of as out-of-control behavior. But *orgia* as it was originally used by Paul is really a state of mind, and the behavior then flows from it.

We do need to stop a minute to clarify the word *anger.* Scripture tells us that anger in itself is not always bad. Anger at unrighteousness, anger on behalf of those who have been hurt or on behalf of the needy or abused can be used of the Spirit to impel us to action. The Lord can use us to better the lives, offer comfort, and bind up the wounds of those people whom Christ loves. Anger can be used righteously, but we are not to allow anger to cause us to sin. Ephesians 4:26–27 admonishes: "And 'don't sin by letting anger control you.' Don't let the sun go down while you are still angry, for anger gives a foothold to the devil" (NLT). Let go of it each day—don't get into bed with it!

There is righteous anger, but then there is that seething anger that can simmer awhile and then boil over like a pot of pasta left cooking on the stove on "high" a minute too long. For months you may have been letting anger simmer inside your mind, and then one evening your spouse does one additional thing, often a small thing. The pot boils over. You release a spray of hot words. They come faster and more furiously as you recite a list of the things from the past six months that your spouse has done that you didn't want him to do, or that he hasn't done and you wanted him to do. The words turn into drops of boiling water that scald and scar. I've been there!

Many of us hold it in and hold it in and hold it in, making that list and checking it twice. That is what this kind of anger is all about. It is about dwelling on those nasty, ugly thoughts. It becomes a state of mind, and it's inevitable that what is inside will eventually boil over and damage all in its path.

In contrast, what does love do? It does not take into account a wrong suffered, whether real or imagined. If we really love our spouses, if we really love our children, if we really love our friends, we turn the stove burner to "off" and we walk away from anger that very day.

7. *We are to take off harsh words.* The New American Standard Bible translates Paul's admonishment this way: "Let all bitterness and wrath and anger and clamor and slander be put away from you, along with all malice" (Eph. 4:30–32). There are differences between "clamor" and "slander." *Clamor,* according to *Webster's,* is "noisy shouting; a loud continuous and insistent noise." Have you ever been in a place where the noise is a constant, relentless din that sets your teeth on edge? Our words should be those of peace, quiet, comfort, and edification, not just words to fill the conversational space.

Slander in the English language means "to defame or malign." Those synonyms are certainly bad enough, but Paul uses the word in the sense of blasphemy, the same word used for blasphemy against the Holy Spirit. When used to describe human relationships, slander is abuse, usually verbal abuse, against someone. It's bearing a false witness or wounding one's reputation through evil reports. It is gossip.

Paul instructs us: "Let everything you say be good and helpful, so that your words will be an encouragement to those who hear them" (Eph. 4:29 NLT). Our words should edify; they should build others up, enlighten, and inform. They should be like seasoning that enhances flavor, enriching the lives and bringing grace to those who hear us.

Florence Littauer, author of *Silver Boxes: The Gift of Encouragement,* speaks and writes about the power of positive words—those that build others up and encourage them. She has said that words are like building blocks.[1] You build others up with the positive things you say. But here's a sobering fact: She says that it takes eleven positive remarks to counteract one negative one. We can take as our personal mission to build our children's self-esteem or to boost our mate's sense of confidence; however, with one thoughtless, negative, hurtful remark, we can knock down those towers we have carefully and lovingly constructed. Harsh, critical, and slanderous words destroy—and we're to be builders, not destroyers.

8. Finally, we're to take off evil behavior. The original word for "evil" here is the same one used in Romans 1:29, in which Paul writes about the behavior of unbelievers: "They are filled with all unrighteousness, evil, greed, and wickedness." Evil refers to ill nature or depravity, given over to a corrupt mind.

As we have reviewed the long list of old garments we are to shed, we need to recognize that this battle is for our minds and our souls, and we determine the outcome. We must realize that the sin we have allowed in our lives is, in the words of Oswald Chambers, "blatant mutiny against God, and either sin or God must die in my life." He continues: "The New Testament brings us right down to this one issue—if sin rules in me, God's life in me will be killed; if God rules in me, sin in me will be killed.

---

1. I heard Mrs. Littauer's building blocks analogy at a conference. Her book on the same subject is listed in the bibliography.

There is nothing more fundamental than that. The culmination of sin was the crucifixion of Jesus Christ, and what was true in the history of God on earth will also be true in your history and in mine—that is, sin will kill the life of God in us."

By our choices we determine our actions and our feelings. We establish the outcome by what we allow to come into our minds and to dwell there. Our minds must be set on Christ. As I list these ugly attitudes and the outcome of our choices, the truth becomes clear: Why would any Christian want to be encumbered by these ugly garments? Hanging on to them is like wearing an old, moth-eaten fur coat from a thrift store in the middle of one of our sweltering Memphis summers. Why would we choose to do that? Take them off!

9
On with the New!

Now you're dressed in a new wardrobe.
Every item of your new way of life is custom-made
by the Creator, with his label on it.
COLOSSIANS 3:10 (MSG)

*E*very little girl dreams of being a princess. She imagines what it will be like when her prince comes for her and sweeps her off her feet, whisking her into happily-ever-after. The Bible says in Ecclesiastes that God has set eternity in our hearts (see Eccles. 3:11). Our own hearts tell us life was intended to be better than this. That is one of the reasons girls and women like "chick flicks" and romance novels. We enjoy a good love story. We want the heroine to marry the hero and for the story to have a happy ending.

Instinctively, we are right. We know we were created for more than this life. The longing for a prince will one day be satisfied when Christ comes for His bride. But until then, we have some work to do. The garments of our old way of life must be taken off and replaced with the garments of a bride—a princess bride—who is preparing for her groom.

The only way we can take off these garments of the old nature and discard them like the rags they are is to *put on our new nature.* Paul says it is an act of our will, to choose to be more like Christ. So *what* do we put on, and *how* do we do it?

There are at least three aspects of Christ's character that we need to put on:

1. We should put on the righteousness of Jesus. The moment we came to Christ He gave us His righteousness. He literally made us the righteousness of God in Christ (2 Cor. 5:21). Take ownership of this righteousness.

2. We should put on holiness. The word *holiness* refers to what our conduct should be if we are joined in fellowship with God. We need to understand the fact that we are holy, set apart by God to walk in newness of life.

3. We should wrap ourselves in truth. *Truth* refers to the unveiled reality of Christ. This truth is actually a transparent cloak. Others should be able to see Jesus Christ in us. Jesus, Himself, is the truth. "But put on the Lord Jesus Christ, and make no provision for the flesh in regard to its lusts" (Rom. 13:14 NASB).

Righteousness, holiness, and truth. These are the "Whats." They describe what we are to put on. The "Hows" point to action. How do we put on these qualities of our new nature? Our new garments must be based on our newness in Christ.

Choose to Confess

We should live with sins confessed. First John 1:9 says, "If we confess our sins, He is faithful and righteous to forgive us our sins and to cleanse us from all unrighteousness" (NASB). God will forgive us. David said in Psalm 32:5, "Then I acknowledged my sin to you and did not cover up my iniquity. I said, 'I will confess my transgressions to the LORD'—and you forgave the guilt of my sin" (NIV). David didn't try to make his own covering; he let God cover his sin.

There is also tremendous power in confessing our sins to each other. James 5:16 says, "Therefore, confess your sins to one another, and pray for one another so that you may be healed. The effective prayer of a righteous man can accomplish much" (NASB). Confessing our sins to a trusted and confidential friend brings what was in the darkness into the light. One of my spiritual mentors, Sylvia Gunter, author of *Prayer Portions* and *Living in His Presence,* once said to me, "The only power the enemy has over a Christian is the power of secrets." What may have seemed insurmountable in the dark will lose its hold over you when it is examined in the light of day and brought before the throne of God.

Choose to Worship

We should come before the Lord in worship and leave our filthy rags at His feet. We must lay down anything we have been carrying or wearing that hinders our worship. Romans 12:1 says, "Therefore I urge you, brethren, by the mercies of God, to present your bodies a living and holy sacrifice, acceptable to God, which is your spiritual service of worship" (Rom. 12:1 NASB). We lay everything on the altar. Nothing is held back!

Choose to Look Up

Here again is Paul's secret to a holy life: "Since, then, you have been raised with Christ, set your hearts on things above, where Christ is seated at the right hand of God. Set your minds on things above, not on earthly things" (Col. 3:1–2 NIV).

By looking up we will have our eyes on what is yet to be—for the glory, the joy that is set before us. We will live this life, run this race faithfully, with our eyes set on Jesus Christ. Paul tells his young protégé Timothy, "Fight the good fight for the faith; take hold of eternal life, to which you were called and have made a good confession before many witnesses" (1 Tim. 6:12).

We must live with an eternal perspective. Mark Buchanan, a pastor in British Columbia, elaborates on our roles and actions this way:

> Live in the light of forever. Choose and think and act now in the light, not of what was, not of what is, but of what is to come. Our future—who we are becoming, where we are going—matters more than our past—where and who we have been. Our future has more power to name us and define us than our past. Consummation swallows origins. Destiny, not history, is the ultimate ground of our identity. How does a prostitute named Rahab, a Moabite outsider named Ruth, an incestuous schemer named Tamar, and an adulteress named Bathsheba, end up in the birth line of Jesus? Because in God's economy the person we become, not the person we have been, is the person we truly are. (162)

Who you are in Christ—holy, righteous, true, blameless, and without spot or wrinkle—is the truth of who you are. Do not listen to anything else, anyone else, anything your past would tell you, or anything the enemy would tell you. You are a child of

God, a daughter of the King of the universe! You have been called to live life on a higher plane and to walk above the circumstances of life with your eyes and your mind set on those things above.

Choose to Renew Your Mind

Paul says, "Do not be conformed to this age, but be transformed by the renewing of your mind, so that you may discern what is the good, pleasing, and perfect will of God" (Rom. 12:2). *Renewing* suggests continuous action. We must continually renew our minds—we shed the old and put on the new and then we shed the old and put on the new—and then we do it again. It's not a one-time action.

This idea reminds me of a friend of mine. She is constantly doing away with the old and putting on the new. Her closet needs a revolving door. She doesn't hesitate to let me know when I need to update my own wardrobe.

We must evaluate our spiritual wardrobe daily. Putting on the new is a process of sanctification. Holiness, with righteousness and truth, are the garments we are to put on. In practical terms, how does this process play out?

When we first make the choice to allow God to sanctify our minds and we start feeding our spirits rather than our flesh, there will be great resistance. Feeding our spirits starts with spending time in God's Word and in prayer. Each of us needs a specific time and a specific place to meet with God. If you choose to meet Him in the morning, you may have a hard time not hitting the snooze button. But if you choose another thirty minutes of sleep, you then miss your quiet time and rush out into your day "undressed." We must also choose to respond instead of react when our husbands are insensitive or our teenagers are belligerent. But choose we must!

Feeding our spirit can cause our flesh to feel neglected at first, and it may scream against the deprivation. If we will keep renewing our minds, however, soon we will look forward to these changes in perspective because they lead to the More that we seek and want to share with others.

Who would want to go back to tension, misery, shame, and guilt? Doing so would be like insisting on putting on that old ratty fur coat that smells of mildew and mothballs. Nobody who is thinking clearly would want to do that. Romans 8:6 says, "The mind-set of the Spirit is life and peace." Nobody whose mind is filled with the truth of God's Word would want to trade her new-found peace for the old turmoil.

Instead, we want to seek what our beloved Peter, after he came to the end of himself, called the "joy inexpressible and full of glory" (1 Pet. 1:8 NASB). Joy has been purchased for us in Christ Jesus. It rightfully belongs to us. It is time to claim it. It is time to say, "Enough of wrong ways of thinking! Enough of the flesh! I'm shedding those old ugly garments! I am choosing to renew my mind."

Choose to Attach Yourself to Jesus

In John 15 Jesus calls Himself the Vine and says that we are the branches. He is the source of our daily spiritual nutrients, our very life source. Our ability to bear fruit comes from the Vine. Have you ever toured a vineyard and noted old tendrils of grapevine that have wound themselves around the wires? The keeper of the vineyard has pruned them away from the vine but has not yet cleared them away. Those old vines are withered and dead. They have no source of food or water anymore. They're just old woody remains of what they once were.

Similarly, apart from our Vine—Jesus Christ—we are nothing. We can do nothing. We can accomplish nothing of eternal significance or bear any fruit apart from Him. We must attach ourselves to Christ.

"Trust in the LORD with all your heart and do not lean on your own understanding. In all your ways acknowledge Him, and He will make your paths straight" (Prov. 3:5–6 NASB). To *trust* means to "attach oneself, confide in, feel safe, and be confident, secure." The word expresses the sense of well-being that results from knowing that the rug won't be pulled out from under you. God is your firm foundation! We can relax when we know who is in control.

Let's take a look at the origin of the word *acknowledge* in Proverbs 3:6. The word evolved from the verb "to admit" and from the noun "knowledge." Together they mean "to admit knowledge of." But there's much more in the word.

In biblical times the word for the verb "to know" also meant "to have sexual intercourse with." Intimacy is implied in *acknowledge.* It is this intimate relationship that is the subject of this entire book. This is the More that will lead us to knowing God like no other. If we acknowledge Him in every area of our lives, He will make our paths straight. He will go before us and prepare the way for us.

Do you want to be free? Then attach yourself to Christ. Determine to know Him intimately. Allow Him to expose anything in your life that is grieving the Holy Spirit. It will be one of the hardest things you have ever done, but it will be the most rewarding pursuit you have ever undertaken. There is nothing like walking intimately with the Lord. There is nothing like walking in freedom with the past forgiven. Once you have forgiven others who have hurt or offended you, you will be free from those old garments of bitterness and unforgiveness. The Holy Spirit will deal with them. The pressure will be off of you.

Forgiveness is not about condoning the sin. It is about being free from the hold it has on you. It is coming to Christ with everything, all the broken pieces of your life. He puts those pieces back together, and then the Holy Spirit comes in and flows through you and becomes your life source.

You will begin to experience a love relationship with Jesus. As a bride dressed in her new, spotless wedding gown you will have eyes only for your Groom. Like the princess in the fairy tales we all loved as children, you will anticipate the arrival of your Prince. As you prepare for His arrival, you will guard your heart because it belongs to Jesus. In *Keeping a Princess Heart in a Not-So-Fairy-Tale World,* Nicole Johnson says, "A Princess heart needs to be guarded, not just grown. A princess is not a commoner, and common things, common relationships, or common deeds are not for her. She must guard her heart against whatever is not worthy, against whatever is not royal or noble, against anything that would discredit her King!" (132).

Once you begin to live as the Beloved of the Lord, it will not be a challenge or a struggle for you to look up as you await your Prince. You will look up because you can't wait to see Him! You have prepared your heart. You are dressed in the garments God designed for you. "Let us rejoice and be glad and give the glory to Him, for the marriage of the Lamb has come and His bride has made herself ready" (Rev. 19:7 NASB).

10

God Fixes Broken Things

The sacrifices of God are a broken spirit,
A broken and a contrite heart—
These, O God, You will not despise.
PSALM 51:17 (NKJV)

*S*wing low, sweet chariot, comin' for to carry me home," sang my daughter and her friends as they acted the parts of Civil War era slaves. As one of the chaperones for the three-day camp, I observed the reenactment of slave trail groups escaping to freedom via the famous Underground Railroad. The "slaves" were each given some forged papers that were their permission to travel under the guise of a touring slave choir. They had to practice the song so they would sound like they really were a choir. The choir also had to rehearse the name of their "master," who had supposedly given his permission for them to travel for a singing engagement. In no way were they to arouse suspicion, and they had to be ready at any moment to show their documents.

The camp counselors dressed in period clothing and met the slaves on the trail. The children had to have their papers with them, and they had to hang onto them tightly. To lose their papers could mean capture, imprisonment, beatings, or even death. They knew their very lives were at stake.

The slaves also had to keep their heads down. They could not look anyone in the eye on the trail because the abolitionists who were trying to help them did not want the slaves to be able to identify them in case the slaves were captured. The slaves had to look down at the ground, always remembering that they were in enemy territory.

Some of the "border patrol" (counselors) would yell at them, with a code word embedded in what they said. The code word was *brother.* If the patrol yelled something like "I am going to get my brother," the slaves knew that the person stopping them was safe. This person would take them to the next stop. Finally, all the trail groups arrived at an open field. Freedom! "Congratulations, you are free, you are free. You have reached the end!" the counselors announced.

I found myself singing "This is how it feels to be free." I think I was as thrilled as they were that they had reached the end of their scary journey.

As Christians, we should also know what it feels like to be free. Our papers have been signed, sealed, and delivered. Yet many times we are satisfied to stay on the plantation—still in slavery, still in bondage, wanting what is on the other side and not realizing it already belongs to us.

Here's the wonderful part: We don't have to look down or back like those slaves had to do. We can look up with the hope of the return of our Savior, who is preparing a place for us and who has promised that He will come again to take us with Him. We are humble, yet we are hopeful as we anticipate what we know awaits us.

Don't Look Back

Remember how the Israelites, wandering in the wilderness, began to look back longingly at their lives of slavery in Egypt? They told each other, "Hey, it wasn't really all that bad!" They complained to Moses and Aaron, "If only we had died by the LORD's hand in the land of Egypt, when we sat by pots of meat and ate all the bread we wanted. Instead, you brought us into this wilderness to make this whole assembly die of hunger!" (Exod. 16:3).

How could they have forgotten that they had been beaten, that they had to fill a daily quota of bricks, that their families were mistreated, and worst of all, that their children were killed? Today, the enemy of God still whispers in our ears, "But wasn't your previous life pretty good, after all? Weren't your needs met?"

God is standing on the edge of our promised land, the Land of More, and He is saying, "Come in, come in." Do not listen to the lies that keep you from experiencing what God has in store for those who love Him. Instead, be like Joshua and Caleb and look forward and upward. We must choose to look up.

Doing so is an act of the will. There are times when our will must be broken. We must come to the end of ourselves so that the Spirit of God can take over. We must no longer will what we desire but our only desire becomes His will. Often that only happens through brokenness.

But wait . . . doesn't brokenness imply a condition of pain? I suspect there are few people who would actually invite pain into their lives—though people often behave in ways that have pain as their consequence for both themselves and others. Pain, though, whether self-caused or not, can lead to dependence on the Lord. And depending on Him leads to the life to which we have been called.

David composed Psalm 51 after he sinned by committing adultery with Bathsheba and having her husband, Uriah, killed. Verses 1 and 2 record his brokenness and repentance: "Have mercy upon me, O God, According to Your lovingkindness; According to the multitude of Your tender mercies, Blot out my transgressions. Wash me thoroughly from my iniquity, And cleanse me from my sin" (NKJV).

He goes on to beseech God to wash him clean: "Behold, you desire truth in the inward parts, And in the hidden part You will make me to know wisdom. Purge me with hyssop, and I shall be clean; Wash me, and I shall be whiter than snow. Make me hear joy and gladness, That the bones You have broken may rejoice. Hide Your face from my sins, And blot out all my iniquities. Create in me a clean heart, O God, And renew a steadfast spirit within me. Do not cast me away from Your presence and do not take your Holy Spirit from me. Restore to me the joy of Your salvation and uphold me by Your generous spirit. Then I will teach transgressors Your ways, And sinners shall be converted to You."

And then he gets specific, referring to the heinous nature of his sin: "Deliver me from the guilt of bloodshed, O God, The God of my salvation, And my tongue shall sing aloud of Your righteousness. O Lord, open my lips, And my mouth shall show forth Your praise. For You do not desire sacrifice, or else I would give it; You do not delight in burnt offering. The sacrifices of

God are a broken spirit, A broken and a contrite heart—These, O God, You will not despise" (NKJV).

David had come to the end of himself, and at that road's end he found new wisdom and understanding of what God really wanted. He realized that God did not want his animal sacrifices, the outward ceremony of confession. The sacrifice God desired was an inward one—a broken and contrite heart.

The words used in the English translation of David's song of repentance reveal much about its meaning. *Broken* literally means "crushed or sorrowful," in other words, penitent—we come to God in repentance, recognizing our sinful condition apart from Him. *Contrite* means "feeling or showing sorrow and remorse for a sin or shortcoming"—that is, not just recognizing our sinfulness but acting upon it in confession. And finally, the *heart* in scriptural terms is the seat of the will. Yes, there's that "will" again. We must surrender our will to God. A broken heart is what He wants—not solemn or fancy formal ceremonies of repentance or grief.

So what are the roadblocks to the end of ourselves? What keeps us from having a broken and contrite heart?

Four Barriers to Brokenness

1. We try to fix the problem ourselves. You might call this the "handyman—or handywoman—technique." Remember Sarah? She got tired of waiting for God's promise that He would make Abraham the father of a great nation. "Aha, God, I know You have promised us a son, but You haven't chosen to open my womb, and now I am too old. I'll take care of this situation myself. I will give my handmaid to my husband, and she can bear a child for us." When we try to fix things ourselves, we often end up with an Ishmael instead of an Isaac. To get God's best, we must wait on Him to act in His own time and in His own way.

2. *We ignore the problem.* I call this "the ostrich technique." If I stick my head in the sand long enough, maybe this issue, this problem, this sin, this stronghold will just pass away and I won't have to deal with it. Part of brokenness is a willingness to confront the sin in our own lives. Sometimes it means speaking the truth in love to a friend or family member. Covering it up or ignoring it is not an option.

3. *We medicate the problem.* This is the "self-help technique." We are hurting, depressed, discouraged, and hopeless. We numb the root cause of our problem with antianxiety medication or antidepressants. We don't deal with the underlying issues. I am not saying there are not medical reasons for these medications. Still, sometimes medication becomes an easy way out instead of taking the time to confront our pain and uncover the "why" of our struggles.

4. *We try to replace the problem.* This might be called "the material girl technique." "If I had another husband, if I just had another job, or if I had that new house, that new sofa, I'd be happy." Sadly, we find that when we get the new husband, the new job, the new house, the new furniture, the issues didn't stay behind. They followed us because they *are* us! It's probably not news to you that statistics show that second marriages are more likely to end in divorce than the first one, especially when children are involved.

We know all too well that none of these fixes work—some of us have been there, done that, tried that, and the results have been pitiful and futile. God's way is to fix *us*—not it or them.

And before He can fix us, He has to break us. How does He do that? How does He bring brokenness into our lives?

Many times the Holy Spirit breaks and purifies us—through trials and suffering. Like Jesus before He was arrested, we must pray: "My Father, if this cannot pass away unless I drink it, Your will be done" (Matt. 26:42 NASB).

When we go through trials and suffering and we allow the Holy Spirit to use His own techniques, not our cheap substitutes, we'll come to the end of ourselves. People will look at us, even in our brokenness, and will be drawn to Jesus in us. They will recognize that we are something other than ordinary. God's Spirit will pour out upon us more and more power, more and more grace. We must allow the Lord to do what only He can do in our lives.

Peter's attitude changed from not wanting to suffer to knowing that suffering leads the Christian to holiness and to a deeper walk with Christ: "You rejoice in this, though now for a short time you have had to be distressed by various trials so that the genuineness of your faith—more valuable than gold, which perishes though refined by fire—may result in praise, glory, and honor at the revelation of Jesus Christ" (1 Pet. 1:6–7).

God Refines Us to Purify Our Faith and Make It Genuine

In her book *As Silver Refined,* Kay Arthur describes the refining process: "And the fire is the fire of His making, for through His fire our Refiner will perfect an awesome work, a divine work. He will take what is impure and make it pure. He will take what is dull and make it beautiful. He'll take what is of potential value and reveal its actual value. He will transform us into a treasure. . . .

Different flames, different fires will come and go. In the pressure of their heat we'll see the impurities in our lives being released and rising to the top. Then He'll skim them off, purifying us, refining us. . . . And all the while, He never leaves or forsakes His treasure. Our Refiner never leaves the crucible, never steps away from the fire" (4).

When we go through the intense heat of trials, if we turn to God, His Word will be used to draw the impurities to the surface so they can be removed. In John 15:3 Jesus says, "You are already clean because of the word I have spoken to you." The Word of God cleanses; in doing so it exposes our thoughts and even our intentions. We are laid bare before the Lord as we read His Word.

So we should embrace our trials. Our question should be: Lord, what are You teaching me in the midst of this? Hebrews 4:12 reinforces this refining process: "For the word of God is living and effective and sharper than any two-edged sword, penetrating as far as to divide soul, spirit, joints, and marrow; it is a judge of the ideas and thoughts of the heart."

God is the Refiner. He purifies us through testing and trials. Sometimes, as we've already discussed, He also allows Satan to sift us. Either way, if we say "Holy Spirit, do Your work in me," we are dying to self. We are choosing to delight ourselves in Him and only in Him.

John 12 tells the rest of the story of Mary of Bethany, sister of Lazarus. She was a woman who demonstrated total submission to her Lord just days before Jesus was crucified. Mary, having died to herself, was let in on the mysteries of God. Somehow she had grasped the truth that Jesus was headed for the cross. She did the most extravagant, even scandalous, thing she could think to do. Smashing open an extremely valuable alabaster vial filled with spikenard, a fragrant and expensive ointment, she anointed Jesus's head and then His feet. Kneeling at His side and taking down her long hair, she used it to wipe His feet. Only a prostitute would have taken her hair down in public! She was willing to humiliate herself to show Jesus that she loved Him. In the only way she could conceive of, she was helping Him bear the pain that was to come. Because of Mary's submission, she had grasped the truth of Christ's impending death. And so she broke open that vial and worshiped Him.

We, too, have a valued vial, or maybe more accurately, each of us *is* a vial. Inside is the sweet fragrance of Christ. But it is only after the vial is broken that others are able to inhale the aroma of Christ. Watchman Nee has some powerful things to say about brokenness in his book *The Release of the Spirit*: "Strange to say, many are still treasuring the alabaster box, thinking that its value exceeds that of the ointment. Many think that their outward man is more precious than their inward man. . . . So the Treasure is in the earthen vessel, but if the earthen vessel is not broken, who can see the Treasure within?" (12–13).

We Must Break the "Me" to Find the More

The breaking of the vial is the breaking of our flesh. This breaking is the death that is required for us to experience a life of More—the resurrection life of Christ. Jesus used a simple metaphor to explain the concept of death preceding life: "Unless a grain of wheat falls into the ground and dies, it remains by itself. But if it dies, it produces a large crop. The one who loves his life will lose it, and the one who hates his life in this world will keep it for eternal life" (John 12:24–25). Luke records more of Jesus's words: "If anyone wants to come with Me, he must deny himself, take up his cross daily, and follow Me" (Luke 9:23).

How does a grain of wheat sprout and grow? It is covered with a husklike hard shell, but when the grain of wheat falls into the earth, it breaks open. The husk is broken and the life is released from inside. It grows into a plant that produces a harvest and more seed so that the next season there is a larger harvest.

The Lord is saying, if you will die, if you will allow Me to break the husk of your flesh open so that the life of the Spirit is released and can flow forth from you, I will make you fruitful. There will be a great harvest not only in your life but in the lives of all you touch.

If the Spirit of God has been released to flow forth from our lives no matter what presses in on us, we will be like Jesus. Watchman Nee describes our new attitude: "Formerly our emotions could be easily aroused, either stirring our love, the most delicate emotion, or provoking our temper, the crudest. But now no matter how many things crowd upon us, our inward man remains unmoved, the presence of God unchanged, and our inner peace unruffled" (25).

Even when the crowd pressed in around Him, Jesus was at peace. When the woman who had been hemorrhaging for twelve years touched His robe, He felt the power flow forth to her, healing her. He was always perceptive of individuals, never in a hurry to move on to someone else, never anxious to get to the next gathering, never frantically trying to check off a to-do list. He was unruffled, and here's why: His mind was stayed on the Father. His mind was set on the truth of what the Father had called Him to do. He was not shaken, even when the crowd clamored to be heard.

Isaiah 26:3 records the song the people of Judah sang as praise for God's spiritual provision: "You will keep in perfect peace the mind [that is] dependent [on You], for it is trusting in You." Another translation puts it this way: "You will keep him in perfect peace, whose mind is stayed on You, because he trusts in You" (NKJV).

Our brokenness is not the end. It is the beginning of His plan for our lives. Relinquish your broken pieces, for it is the Father's delight to make you into the image of His dear Son.

11

Know Your Enemy

A thief comes only to steal and to kill and to destroy.
JOHN 10:10a

I played varsity girls basketball in high school. One of the things our coach would have us do was to study our opponents. We would scout them at games. One of our objectives was to analyze the strengths and weaknesses of the person we would be guarding. Winning was more likely if we knew the playing style of the other team.

If you have been a Christian for very long, you realize that we have a very real enemy, and we do need to know who we're dealing with. The Bible uses many different descriptions and names for him (the words below are from the NASB):

- He is *crafty.* "The serpent was more crafty than any beast of the field which the LORD God had made" (Gen. 3:1).
- He is a *deceiver.* He deceived Eve, and he continues to deceive us. "But I am afraid that, as the serpent deceived Eve by his craftiness, your minds will be led astray from the simplicity and purity of devotion to Christ" (2 Cor. 11:3).

- He is the *tempter* (Matt. 4:3; 1 Thess. 3:5).
- He is the ruler of the demons, *Beelzebul* (Matt. 12:24).
- He is a *murderer* (John 8:44).
- He is a *liar and the father of lies* (John 8:44).
- He is the *evil one* (John 17:15).
- He is the *god of this world* (2 Cor. 4:4).
- He sometimes disguises himself as an *angel of light* (2 Cor. 11:14).
- He is the *prince of the power of the air* (Eph. 2:2).
- He is *Satan* (Mark 1:13).
- He is the *dragon,* "the serpent of old who is called the devil and Satan, who deceives the whole world" (Rev. 12:7–9).
- He is the *accuser* (Rev. 12:10) who accuses us before the Father night and day.

And this is not an exhaustive list!

God has an awesome plan for your life—"plans for [your] welfare, not for disaster, to give you a future and a hope," says Jeremiah 29:11. However, Satan has an alternate plan. Satan's plan is to kill, steal, and destroy. He is *scheming* against us (see Eph. 6:11). The word for *schemes* (NASB) can also be translated "wiles" (KJV) or "strategies" (NLT). The word in the Greek is *methodeia,* from which we get the word *method.*

In her book *When Godly People Do Ungodly Things,* Beth Moore states: "The most obvious word found in the Greek is *method.* If we could only understand that the devil does not work haphazardly but carefully, methodically, weaving and spinning, and watching for just the right time. He truly has a method to his madness. He draws out plans and executes them very carefully. He carefully sets traps for the express purpose of wreaking destruction in the lives of the saints" (81). That is why God gives us armor that we might stand firm and resist the evil one.

One of the most vivid pictures of how Satan operates is recorded for us in Genesis 4, the account of Cain and Abel and their offerings. God had regard for Abel and his offering because Abel brought of the firstlings of his flock, the best. Scripture states that Cain simply brought an offering from the fruit of the ground, and God did not show favor to Cain for his offering. This made Cain very angry. The Lord said to Cain, "Why are you furious? And why are you downcast? If you do right, won't you be accepted? But if you do not do right, sin is crouching at the door. Its desire is for you, but you must master it" (Gen. 4:6–7).

The Lord chose some interesting words to describe the sin that was lurking at Cain's door. To *crouch* means to "lie in wait in a place of concealment, especially for an evil purpose." Can't you just see the enemy as the lion described in 1 Peter 5:8? The Lord penned through Peter: "Be sober! Be on the alert! Your adversary the Devil is prowling around like a roaring lion, looking for anyone he can devour." This verse tells us that Satan's yearning, his desire, is for us—quite literally.

But just as the Lord instructed Cain, we too must master sin. To *master* means to "rule, to govern, to have dominion over." We can do that! We live on this side of the cross, and we have been given dominion over the enemy. Ephesians 2:6 tells us that God has "seated us with Him in the heavenly places in Christ Jesus" (NASB). How much higher could we get? The answer is this: We're there both now and in eternity, thanks to Christ's sacrifice.

Think of Jesus As the Lion Tamer Who Puts the Enemy under Subjection

Because Satan was defeated by Jesus on Calvary, he is now in subjection to Him. He has always been on a leash (look at how God handled him with Job), and he still is. As I reflected on this mental image, I began drawing in my journal. I drew a cage with bars and rejoiced that the enemy has been forced into it.

So, if he is a defeated enemy, why do so many Christians allow him, instead, to defeat them? All too often we open the door to the cage. We give him legal rights to our lives every time we give in to sin. Ephesians 4:26–27 says, "Be angry and yet do not sin; do not let the sun go down on your anger, and do not give the devil an opportunity" (NASB). The word for "opportunity" in the Greek is *topos,* which means "place" or "ground." Our word *topography,* the mapping of actual physical characteristics of a place, comes from *topos.* The word means we are not to give the devil a foothold or ground in our lives through sin.

A friend had been having some of the same thoughts about the devil and had written them down in a note that her husband handed to me at church one Sunday. You can imagine my excitement when I read her description of Jesus as the lion tamer! Have you ever been to the circus and seen a lion tamer at work? When we confess our sin and call on our Savior for forgiveness, He cracks His whip and forces the lion back into his cage. Jesus has the lion under control and will keep him at bay until he is destroyed forever.

Now there are times that the Lord allows the enemy to come against us when we have no knowledge of unconfessed sin in our lives. It is during these times that the Lord is testing us and refining us to make us more like Jesus. But we must be careful that we don't allow Satan to deceive us, "having been held captive to do his will" (2 Tim. 2:26 NASB).

We know that Satan's desire is to steal, kill, and destroy (see John 10:10a). He wants to come in and destroy your marriage. He would love to destroy your relationship with your children and your friends. He is especially wreaking havoc in bodies of Christ through division and separation. He is bent on bringing destruction into your life.

The Weapons You Have Are Made of the Best Materials

We have been given weapons. They are not of the flesh, they are not tangible, they are spiritual—but make no mistake, they are real! These weapons are to protect us from the enemy and to enable us to tear down the strongholds, those wrong ways of thinking that Satan uses against all of us.

The Message puts Ephesians 6:10–18 into this contemporary language:

> God is strong, and he wants you strong. So take everything the Master has set out for you, well-made weapons of the best materials. And put them to use so you will be able to stand up to everything the Devil throws your way. This is no afternoon athletic contest that we'll walk away from and forget about in a couple of hours. This is for keeps, a life-or-death fight to the finish against the Devil and all his angels. Be prepared. You're up against far more than you can handle on your own. Take all the help you

can get, every weapon God has issued, so that when it is all over but the shouting you will still be on your feet. Truth, righteousness, peace, faith, and salvation are more than words. Learn how to apply them. You will need them throughout your life. God's Word is an indispensable weapon. In the same way, prayer is essential in this ongoing warfare. Pray hard and long. Pray for your brothers and sisters. Keep your eyes open. Keep each other's spirits up so that no one falls behind or drops out.

We live in hostile territory, with a very real and present enemy. We must be alert and equipped. That is why we study the Word of God, pray, listen to sermons and teachings from God's Word, and read Christian books. All of these activities strengthen us spiritually and prepare us to use our spiritual weapons.

We must be prepared! We can pretend that the war isn't raging around us, but the signs are too evident to ignore.

We have three options:

Option 1: We can hide behind unbelief and denial. We can get into the foxhole of pretense, hunkering down, hiding our eyes from the evil of the world. This method doesn't work with ignoring our own sin through the "ostrich approach," as we've already suggested, and it doesn't work any better in ignoring the enemy. We can hope that the war will pass over us and we will be unaffected. But when we live in denial, we leave ourselves wide open for the advancement of the enemy. We are not appropriating the weapons that the Lord has provided so we can stand against the onslaught.

Option 2: We can grit our teeth and try to utilize our own resources. This sounds like a good plan, but Satan is a much too difficult foe for us. The only way we can fight him is in the Spirit. If we go out using our own resources, we will be like a lone soldier standing in the middle of a wide desert, an easy target for the enemy or his minions. We will fall into a trap or snare hidden in the sand, and he will take us down. He will come in and steal from us, and he will seek to destroy not only our personal lives but the lives of those we love as well.

Option 3 (the only viable one): We must take up the whole armor of God and stand firm. We must wield the Sword of the Spirit and put prayer to use, entering into the spirit realm to do battle with the enemy of our souls. It is here that we can follow the admonition of Paul: "We are destroying speculations and every lofty thing raised up against the knowledge of God, and we are taking every thought captive to the obedience of Christ" (2 Cor. 10:5 NASB). We tear down those counterfeit strongholds and take captive the lies we have believed and that the enemy has hidden behind. In their place, we begin to erect strongholds of truth.

Many times the lies we have allowed to define us are difficult to remove. Sometimes they have been a part of us for so long that we feel as if they *are* us. If we have been harboring unforgiveness, we may recall the original wound and relive all of the old emotions, believing that we have a right to harbor these feelings, especially the anger and bitterness that is directed toward the offender.

When we do this, however, we become like the woman in an old story who contacted a local artist to have her portrait painted. She told the artist that she had a very important piece of jewelry that she wanted to wear. The jewelry was a brooch that had been passed down through her family for generations and was very important to her. She wore it around her neck on a chain. She told the artist she was very proud of it and that it was worth a lot of money.

The artist said, "Yes, that's fine. I'll paint you wearing it." He didn't really understand her emphasis on the brooch, but he thought if it was that important to her, he would put it in the portrait.

The woman walked in the day of her sitting, and as she entered the artist's studio, he looked at her and was appalled. There was not a brooch around her neck; it was a roach!

Many times, we are like the woman in that story. We may have sin patterns that have been passed down through our family, and we think, *This is just the way I am.* For instance, we may say, "My family members are all worriers; that's just the way we are." Or, we hold a grudge because "that's just how we are." But if we could see our sin the way God sees it, we would react to it much like we would to a roach on our body. We would grasp it and cast it away from us without hesitation. We would see it for what it is: filthy, disgusting, and potentially deadly. Like the roach that can carry deadly disease, sin will kill not only our souls and spirits but also our bodies if it is not brought to the cross.

We must ask the Lord to allow us to see our sin the way He sees it. We can't continue to hide it, coddle it, or suppress it. We must allow the Lord to dig up the fallow ground and expose anything in our lives that doesn't glorify Jesus Christ. Much as a tourniquet stops blood from flowing, unconfessed sin can hinder or quench the flow of the Holy Spirit in our lives and steal the abundant life that Jesus died to give us.

What we are being called on to do will not be easy. Death to the flesh never is. *The battle is real.*

In 1836, General William Barret Travis and his men were fighting for the freedom of Texas from Mexico. The Mexican army had captured San Antonio. Volunteers were coming in to help the Texans take back the Alamo. There were only 189 Texan volunteers against about 2,000 Mexican soldiers. These 189 men held off the Mexican army for thirteen days. General Travis sent out the following letter on February 24, 1836, asking for reinforcements from all the areas around Texas and other parts of the United States. This letter became known as the "Travis letter."[1]

To the people of Texas
and all Americans in the world.

Fellow citizens and compatriots:

I am besieged, by a thousand or more of the Mexicans under Santa Anna—I have sustained a continual bombardment and cannonade for 24 hours and have not lost a man—The enemy has demanded a surrender at discretion, otherwise, the garrison are to be put to the sword, if the fort is taken—I have answered the demand with a cannon shot, and our flag still waves proudly from the walls—*I shall never surrender or retreat.* Then, I call on you in the name of Liberty, of patriotism, and every thing dear to the American character, to come to our aid, with all dispatch—The enemy is receiving reinforcements daily and will no doubt increase to three or four thousand in four or five days. If this call is

---

1. Only minor changes have been made for capitalization and punctuation. See http://www.ntanet.net/travis.html.

neglected, I am determined to sustain myself as long as possible and die like a soldier who never forgets what is due to his own honor and that of his country.

VICTORY OR DEATH

William Barret Travis
Lt. Col. Comdt.

P. S. The Lord is on our side.

Legend has it that when it appeared that the reinforcements would not get there in time, General Travis drew a line in the dirt and had all the men line up. He said, "If you are willing to go down with me, if you are willing to fight to the finish, step over the line." All of the men but two stepped over that line. William Barret Travis was only twenty-six years old, showing amazing bravery for such a young man. Those 189 men held off the Mexican army for thirteen days. On March 6, 1836, the Mexican army overtook the Alamo.

But just two months later the forces were ordered out of Texas after Santa Anna was captured at the Battle of San Jacinto. Santa Anna's losses were estimated at 600 men. The cry of the battle for the freedom of Texas became "Remember the Alamo!" It rallied the forces. It became the cry from the lips of all the troops who were willing to lay lives on the line for freedom. The Alamo was retaken, and the freedom of Texas was secured.

David Jett, a friend and former associate pastor, rewrote the famous Travis letter for modern-day believers:[2]

---

2. Unpublished letter used with permission of the writer.

Fellow strangers and aliens in this world:

I am besieged, by Satan and his demons. I have sustained a continual bombardment through his accusations, temptations, and insinuations. The Enemy has demanded a surrender; otherwise, I am to be put to the sword if the fort is taken. I have answered the demand with the sword of the Spirit, the Word of God! *I shall never surrender or retreat!* I call on you in the name of the Lord Jesus Christ, to join me in this battle of the ages. The Enemy is receiving reinforcements daily. If this call is neglected, I am determined to sustain myself as much as possible and die like a soldier of the cross who never forgets what is dear to his own honor and that of his Savior.

Give me VICTORY or give me DEATH.

The Overcoming Christian

The Lord has given us a battle cry today: "Remember Calvary!" May it be our rallying call-to-arms as we walk through this dark world. It is time for every Christian, every blood-bought child of God, to stand up and be counted. It's time to get out of the foxhole and quit trying to live this life on our own. We must quit falling into the traps and snares of the enemy. We must no longer stand unprotected, vulnerable to attack, but must put on the whole armor of God and stand firm against the enemy's schemes.

It is time to count for Christ. He has drawn a line in the sand. Are you willing to step over? It's time to do battle!

The following is a prayer to prepare your heart for the chapters to come. We will be dealing with specific areas of sin that the enemy uses to erect strongholds in our lives. Remember, the Lord is looking at your heart.

> *Dear Heavenly Father,*
> *Through the power of Your Holy Spirit, I am ready*
> *to take my stand alongside the great warriors of the faith.*
> *Lord, expose any deception or unperceived sin in my life.*
> *Fill me with your Holy Spirit. Prepare me for battle.*
> *This battle begins with an act of my will. I choose to deny*
> *myself, take up my cross, and follow Christ. Lead me and*
> *direct me as I deal with specific sins. Help me to be the*
> *overcomer Christ died to make me. I confess that You are*
> *my Lord and Master!*
> *In Jesus's name, Amen.*[3]

---

3. See Ps. 139, Eph. 3:18, Eph. 5:10, and Luke 9:23 for source material related to this prayer.

12

Forgiveness
Is a Choice

For if you forgive others for their transgressions,
your heavenly Father will also forgive you.
MATTHEW 6:14 (NASB)

*O*ne of the most difficult issues we all deal with is forgiveness. As women, God created us as relational creatures. Relationships are closely related to our self-esteem. Close friends have access to our heart in ways that leave us vulnerable to experiencing pain. Several years ago I was deeply hurt by someone very close to me. It was a betrayal that inflicted a deep wound. I remember going into my bedroom to be alone with the Lord. I knelt in front of my chair, laid my head on the seat, and began to weep and cry out to the Lord: "Oh, Lord, this is so painful. I never thought this person would do something like this. This isn't fair; it isn't right. I don't deserve this!"

About the time those words came out of my mouth, I sensed that still small voice of the Holy Spirit say, "You're right. You don't deserve this. You deserve hell, just like everyone does."

I just wilted before Him! I said, "Lord, how self-righteous of me. How judgmental of me! Father, forgive me for my own sin and help me to choose forgiveness."

When we look at the Lord's Prayer, or what might be more accurately called the Model Prayer, we see the teaching of Jesus on forgiveness. He told His disciples to pray in this way: "Forgive us our debts, as we also have forgiven our debtors" (Matt. 6:12). Jesus went on to say, "For if you forgive others for their transgressions, your heavenly Father will also forgive you. But if you do not forgive others, then your Father will not forgive your transgressions" (Matt. 6:14–15 NASB).

When We Forgive, We Are Also Forgiven

According to Jesus, if we want to be forgiven, we must forgive. It is sometimes necessary to start with this ulterior motive as our first step. We choose to forgive so that we will personally be forgiven. After we have taken this initial step of obedience, the Lord will then enable us to move on to true forgiveness, which is from the heart. Matthew 18 recounts Jesus's familiar parable of the servant who owed his master an amount that would be equivalent to millions of dollars today. The servant had no way to repay the debt, so the master commanded that he be sold along with his wife, his children, and all his possessions. The servant prostrated himself before the king, begging him, "Have patience with me and I will repay you everything" (v. 26 NASB). The king felt compassion for the man's plight and released him and forgave him the debt.

But that slave went out and found a fellow slave who owed him a hundred *denari*—a denari was equivalent to about one day's wages for a laborer—and seized him. He began to choke the other man, demanding, "Pay me back what you owe" (v. 28).

The fellow slave begged him to have patience. He promised to repay everything, but his cries were wasted. The slave whose debt had been canceled was unwilling to forgive the fellow slave's debt to him. He had the man thrown into prison until he paid back what was owed.

When the other slaves saw what had happened, they were deeply saddened and reported to their lord all that had happened. Summoning the slave, the king said to him, "You wicked slave, I forgave you all that debt because you pleaded with me. Should you not also have had mercy on your fellow slave, in the same way that I had mercy on you?" (vv. 32–33). The angry king handed the slave over to the torturers until he should repay all that he owed the king. Jesus ends the account, "My heavenly Father will also do the same to you, if each of you does not forgive his brother from the heart" (v. 35).

This wicked slave owed an astronomical sum of money, and his fellow slave owed him what would have been miniscule in comparison. Do you see yourself in this parable?

To be honest, I see myself. I was the one who owed the millions. I was the one who owed a debt there was no way I could pay. And I prostrated myself, coming to the cross and asking for the Father's forgiveness and for salvation in Jesus's name.

Yet like the wicked slave, we may have harbored unforgiveness toward someone over a negligible debt. We have been unwilling to take out our mental ledger book and draw a big black line through the debt. We may have taken into account every wrong suffered and marked an "amount due" next to the calculations! When we do not forgive, the Lord will turn to us, just as He did to the slave, and say, "You wicked servant!" He will then hand us over to the torturers.

How so? In what way does God hand us over? When we harbor unforgiveness, we continue to relive the offense and to dwell on it. The offense taunts and tortures us, replaying over and over in our minds. Choosing unforgiveness opens a door to the enemy. He then comes in and builds a stronghold, piling on top of the unforgiveness more stones of deception, lies, anger, and bitterness.

In Mark 11:25–26 Jesus said, "Whenever you stand praying, forgive, if you have anything against anyone, so that your Father who is in heaven will also forgive you your transgressions. But if you do not forgive, neither will your Father who is in heaven forgive your transgressions" (NASB). Unforgiveness causes us not to be forgiven. It prevents our prayers from being heard (Ps. 66:18) and causes a root of bitterness to spring up that "defiles many" (Heb. 12:15). Some of you may be thinking, *Yes, but you have no idea what he/she did to me. What happened to me is too terrible to forgive.* I'm sure what has happened to some of you is horrific! But are you willing to continue torturing yourself and giving the enemy the advantage just so you can hold on to the offense?

When We Forgive, We Are Healed

What happens when we forgive our offenders? We set ourselves free. We don't wait until we are healed to forgive. We forgive so that we can be healed. The Lord begins to heal us through the power of His Spirit as we step out by faith in obedience.

In her book *Praying God's Word,* Beth Moore states: "Innumerable strongholds are connected to an unwillingness to forgive. Left untreated, unforgiveness becomes spiritual cancer.

Bitterness takes root and since the root feeds the rest of the tree, every branch of our lives and each limb ultimately becomes poisoned. Beloved sister or brother, the bottom line is unforgiveness makes us sick, always spiritually, often emotionally and surprisingly often physically" (220).

Forgiveness is not denying what happened. It is not saying that what happened didn't hurt. In fact, in her chapter on forgiveness, Beth suggests that we go to the Lord and pour our hearts out to Him. He knows what happened—it grieved Him as well. Tell on them! David did. Look at his psalms. He was brutally honest as he poured out his heart before the Lord. He spoke openly of his enemies. And yet God said that David was "a man after his own heart" (1 Sam. 13:14 NIV). Job also cried out to God, and God Himself said that "Job did not sin with his lips" (Job 2:10 NASB).

May I just say this: You will never *feel* like forgiving. But *choose* forgiveness. Your flesh will never allow you to feel like forgiving. We choose as an act of our will to forgive. We must choose it every day. Each time an old feeling of anger or bitterness resurfaces, we must give it to Jesus and choose to forgive.

Here's what will happen: There will come a day when we will think of the offense or betrayal and suddenly realize that the Lord has done just what we asked Him to do. He erased the pain from our hearts and minds, allowing us to feel love and compassion for the one who brought so much pain. That is a miracle, a supernatural grace gift of the Lord. It is the beginning of understanding the *agape* love of God.

It's what happened to me when I turned over the pain of betrayal inflicted by my friend to my loving Father. In fact, almost every time I try to harbor unforgiveness, the Lord gives me a good look at my own sin. He shows me my own need for forgiveness, my need for the Savior, my desperate condition apart from Him. How can I offer anything less than what He has so freely given me in Christ Jesus? How can any of us?

Forgiveness does not mean that you immediately forget the offense. Many times people will say, mistakenly, "You have to forgive and forget." God doesn't forget our sin. He forgives our sin and chooses to no longer hold it against us.

Applying forgiveness to our own behavior toward others does not mean denying that the wrong or the hurt happened. It is not saying that what the person did was not wrong. Here's what it is: It's taking the person off your hook and putting him or her on the Lord's. "Never take your own revenge, beloved, but leave room for the wrath of God, for it is written, 'Vengeance is mine, I will repay,' says the Lord" (Rom. 12:19 NASB).

As you choose forgiveness, you will find that your prayers will begin to change. You may start off praying "about" a person but find that soon you begin to pray "for" the person. Scripture tells us that we are to love our enemies and to bless those who curse us: "But if your enemy is hungry, feed him, and if he is thirsty, give him a drink; for in so doing you will heap burning coals on his head" (Rom. 12:20 NASB). We are never more like Jesus than when we choose to walk in forgiveness.

When We Send an SOS to God, He Helps Us Forgive

Evelyn Christenson is a woman who has greatly impacted my life through her writings. She is the author of *What Happens When Women Pray, Gaining Through Losing,* and many others. I attended two of her conferences and marked the verses in my Bible that she had claimed as her "SOS verses." She says when someone hurts her, maybe through something they said, she immediately sends up an SOS. Her SOS is: "So, as those who have been chosen of God, holy and beloved, put on a heart of compassion, kindness, humility, gentleness and patience; bearing with one another, and forgiving each other, whoever has a complaint against anyone; just as the Lord forgave you, so also should you" (Col. 3:12–13 NASB). You may even want to mark these verses in your Bible with an "SOS" beside them. They would be great verses to memorize and utilize in your sword-wielding with the enemy.

What is the result if we don't choose forgiveness? Unforgiveness will many times manifest itself as anger and bitterness. Do you remember the anger of Cain? It went from intense anger to bitterness, to a desire for revenge, to murder. Unforgiveness is the stuff of which hatred and murder are made. That is why we must be ruthless about ripping it from our lives.

The Lord has much to say about anger—the selfish kind, the prideful kind, the "me, me, me" kind. There are many passages that expose the folly of anger:

- "A fool's anger is known at once, but a prudent man conceals dishonor" (Prov. 12:16 NASB). A wise person ignores the insults of others.
- "He who is slow to anger has great understanding, but he who is quick tempered exalts folly" (Prov. 14:29 NASB).
- "A gentle answer turns away wrath, but a harsh word stirs up anger" (Prov. 15:1 NASB).
- We are told not to even associate with a man "given to anger, or go with a hot tempered man, or you will learn his ways and find a snare for yourself" (Prov. 22:24–25 NASB).

- "Do not be eager in your heart to be angry, for anger resides in the bosom of fools" (Solomon's words in Eccles. 7:9 NASB).

These verses tell us that if we want to be wise, we will choose to be long-suffering like our Lord. If we trust the Lord with all of our hearts, He will make our path straight or peaceful as He tells us in Proverbs 3:5–6.

In Galatians 5:20, anger ("fits of rage" in the NIV) is listed as one of the deeds of the flesh, of our old nature. It is one of the old garments described in Ephesians 4:17–32 that we are to put off like that old moth-infested coat that smells of dust and mold.

The Bible tells us that if we continue to practice these deeds of the flesh (HCSB lists them as "sexual immorality, moral impurity, promiscuity, idolatry, sorcery, hatreds, strife, jealousy, outbursts of anger, selfish ambitions, dissensions, factions, envy, drunkenness, carousing") and are not convicted by the Lord, it is evident that we do not belong to Him. Scripture is very clear that those who live in these habitual sin patterns "will not inherit the kingdom of God" (Gal. 5:19–21). The warning could hardly be stronger.

We've previously looked into Ephesians 4. At the end of this chapter Paul gives us some instructions: "Let no unwholesome word proceed from your mouth, but only such a word as is good for edification according to the need of the moment, so that it will give grace to those who hear. Do not grieve the Holy Spirit of God, by whom you were sealed for the day of redemption. Let all bitterness and wrath and anger and clamor and slander be put away from you, along with all malice" (Eph. 4:29–31 NASB).

The Lord is saying through Paul, if you get angry, deal with it. If someone has hurt you, confront him or her in love. Seek restoration in the relationship, not blame. If you have hurt someone else, go to that person in love and ask for forgiveness. We can choose forgiveness, but we cannot force someone else to forgive. How he or she chooses to respond is between that person and the Lord. "If possible, so far as it depends on you, be at peace with all men" (Rom. 12:18 NASB).

When We Do Not Forgive, We Cannot Walk in the Spirit

A woman in a Bible study I was teaching came to me one day with a prayer request. She had a group of friends who had always done everything together. One of them had gotten angry at her, and they had gone for several months without talking. The whole group had been at odds with one another. They had allowed the sun to go down on their anger, and the devil had taken advantage. Now their group of friends was divided. I listened to her and then told her she knew what the Lord required of her. She needed to go to these friends and apologize for however she had hurt or offended them and ask for their forgiveness. She needed to tell them that their friendship meant more to her than this offense.

She did just that. But one of the young women said, "I forgive you, but I still don't want to be friends with you." This revealed more about that young woman's spiritual condition than she wanted to reveal. She was not walking in the Spirit. But the woman who apologized was freed from responsibility. She had done what the Lord asked of her. She was free to "present her gift at the altar" (see Matt. 5:23).

In his chapter on forgiveness in *Reclaiming Surrendered Ground,* Jim Logan instructs readers to write down the names of people against whom they are holding feelings of unforgiveness:

"Make a list of the name(s) as God reveals them. Also, check yourself to see if you are holding any bitterness toward God or yourself, and include these names on your list if that is the case." He then instructs the reader to start at the bottom of the list and to forgive each one. You start at the bottom because those are usually the ones who are easier to forgive. As you work your way up the list, release each person and offense to the Lord. "If after forgiving the person for the major offense you recall a specific, hurtful incident, don't let your feelings smolder anew. Instead, release them to God then and there," he counsels (64).

This is the beginning of forgiveness. We must choose it on a daily basis. If the enemy taunts you with a past painful memory, you must surrender it to the Lord immediately and choose forgiveness once again—and then again the next time. Remember, we who have been forgiven a debt we could never repay cannot offer anything less than full forgiveness to others.

Why don't you stop right now? Lay this book down and make your list. Follow Logan's suggestion and start at the bottom of your list and work your way to the top. This is an act of your will in obedience to God's command. Here is a suggested prayer to help you follow through:

Dear Father,

I confess that I have been harboring unforgiveness that has turned into bitterness. I ask You to forgive me. Lord, as I lift each of these offenses up to You, I am choosing to obey You. Father, I forgive _____ for _____ _____. In the name of Jesus, I choose forgiveness. [Do this or something similar for each of the people and offenses on your list.]

In Jesus's name, Amen.

13

It's Not about Me!

For everyone who exalts himself will be humbled,
and the one who humbles himself will be exalted.

LUKE 14:11

Our youngest daughter, Bethany, played the part of Louisa, one of the Von Trapp children, in a school production of *The Sound of Music.* If you've seen the play yourself or the film version of it, do you remember how cute Maria was as she summoned up her courage to meet Captain Von Trapp and his children for the first time? Dressed in her shabby outfit, she sang "I have confidence in me!" at the top of her voice! But when we think about her words, we realize they were not really so cute. Too often our confidence is placed in our abilities instead of in the Lord.

Many times pride will be what keeps us from choosing forgiveness. Trusting self leads to pride, which is a sin that goes back to the beginning of time and before. In fact, pride started with the enemy of our souls. Isaiah depicts God's account of the fall of Lucifer, or Satan: "How you have fallen from heaven, O star of the morning, son of the dawn! You have been cut down to the earth, you who have weakened the nations! But you said in your heart, '*I* will ascend to heaven; *I* will raise my throne above the stars of God, and *I* will sit on the mount of assembly in the recesses of the north. *I* will ascend above the heights of the clouds; *I* will make myself like the Most High.' Nevertheless you will be thrust down to Sheol, to the recesses of the pit" (Isa. 14:12–15 NASB, emphasis mine).

Notice the five "I will" statements that the enemy made. He was saying, *I* will be God! When we allow pride to rule and reign in our lives, we line up with the enemy because, like the father of lies, we are saying, "I will be God! I will be in control." The great Victorian evangelical theologian J. C. Ryle once said, "Of all the doctrines of the Bible, none is so offensive to human nature as the doctrine of God's Sovereignty."

Ezekiel 28:14–17 also describes Satan and his fall. These verses tell us that Satan was in the Garden of Eden. He was full of wisdom and beauty, covered with jewels and gold:

"You were the anointed cherub who covers, and I placed you there. You were on the holy mountain of God; you walked in the midst of the stones of fire. You were blameless in your ways from the day you were created *until unrighteousness was found in you.* By the abundance of your trade you were internally filled with violence, and you sinned; therefore I have cast you as profane from the mountain of God. And I have destroyed you, O covering cherub, from the midst of the stones of fire. *Your heart was lifted up because of your beauty; you corrupted your wisdom by reason of your splendor.*" (NASB, emphasis mine)

There Are Two Different Choices—
God's Will or My Will

We forfeit the presence of God when we allow pride to sit on the throne. "God is opposed to the proud, but gives grace to the humble," says James 4:6b (NASB). Going our own way always leads to the snare of the enemy, and we end up suffering from the harvest of the seeds we have sown. Sin will always take us further than we planned to go and cost us more than we wanted to pay. We will end up self-destructing if we don't turn back to the Lord.

What does God say about pride and those who are proud?

- "Everyone who is proud in heart is an abomination to the LORD; assuredly he will not be unpunished" (Prov. 16:5 NASB).
- "Pride goes before destruction, and a haughty spirit before stumbling" (Prov. 16:18 NASB).
- "A man's pride will bring him low, but a humble spirit will obtain honor" (Prov. 29:23 NASB).

In *Reclaiming Surrendered Ground,* Jim Logan says, "When we let pride come into our lives, God withholds spiritual power. And as we read in Proverbs, after pride comes a fall. The enemy brings in a destructive temptation which is too strong for us to handle, and without God's power we fall" (89).

To deal with pride, we need a radical redirection of our focus. God's antidote for pride is humility. Andrew Murray's definition of humility is my favorite: "The humble person is not one who thinks meanly (poorly) of himself, he simply does not think of himself at all" (quoted by Michael Green, *Illustrations for Biblical Preaching*, 200).

Instead of thinking about ourselves, Paul tells us what to do: "Keep seeking the things above, where Christ is, seated at the right hand of God" (Col. 3:1 NASB). If we choose to focus on Christ and submit to Him in every area of our lives, we are telling Him we want to live our lives *for Him and His way.* That leaves no room for elevating our own way of thinking above the Word of God.

Besides, if I have been crucified with Christ, I am dead! Dead men and women can't get their feelings hurt. Dead men and women can't think highly of themselves—they're dead! How often we profess death to the flesh but allow an area of our lives to remain uncrucified!

When I was preparing to teach a session on pride a few years ago, I couldn't seem to finish the outline for it. I kept going to my knees and then falling on my face in prayer. The Lord began to deal with me in His gentle way. I sensed Him teaching me: "Donna, in so many ways, you still want your own way. At so many turns you want what you want." I know that's true.

There Are Two Forces At War—God and Self

When things don't go my way, too often I find myself mumbling and grumbling like the Israelites did in the wilderness. I have to stop myself and intentionally submit to the Lord and choose Him. In his book *Deliver Me,* Richard Exley explains that "there is only one temptation, the ever-present temptation to choose my will over God's will, my way over God's way. At the root of every spiritual struggle, there are two forces at war; not so much good and evil, but God and self" (17). I have certainly found this to be an accurate description of my own life.

Jesus put our actions into straightforward words: "And He was saying to them all, 'If anyone wishes to come after Me, let him deny himself and take up his cross daily and follow Me'" (Luke 9:23 NASB). I wish I could tell you that this struggle is a once-and-for-all battle, that you can lay the ax to the root of pride and be done with it. Unfortunately, the root is connected to the fallen nature of our flesh, and it springs back up overnight. That is why we must daily mortify—from the Latin word *mors,* or "death"—put to death the flesh. I see an unintentional (or maybe not so unintentional) ironic play on words in *mors*;—while it means "death," it leads to life—and More.

There will be days when you won't feel like dying to your desires and will perhaps find yourself falling prey to making decisions based on feelings. Being aware of the danger is the first step. Knowing what the truth of God's Word says, we make decisions based on His Word and not our feelings. We must will to set our minds on Christ and His Word, and as we do, our right thinking will change our actions, and our feelings will eventually follow.

First Peter 5:6–7 says, "Humble yourselves under the mighty hand of God, that He may exalt you at the proper time" (NASB). We don't have to look to our own pride for self-validation.

And that's a comfort because pride does not validate—it puffs up, like a bloated, overfed, and sickly fish in a dirty aquarium. There is nothing beautiful or glorifying about it. It is ugly and destructive in its manifestations and in what it leads to in our relationships with God and with others.

Why is pride so ugly? Because it leads to rebellion. Anytime I go my own way, I am rebelling against God. I am choosing to go the way of Satan. I am choosing to say, "I have this one under control, God. I know how to handle this." I am saying that I want to be in control.

The English word *rebellion* has embedded in it two words, and in a Christian context, both exude danger. *Rebel* is both a verb and a noun. If I go my own way—if I rebel—I am a rebel. Remove the word *rebel* from *rebellion* and what is left? *Lion.* I am convinced that this lion is that "roaring lion, seeking someone to devour" that 1 Peter 5:8 (NASB) describes. I am never more like the lion than when I rebel from what I know God wants me to do, choosing to go my own way. I go against what I know is true to satisfy my flesh. Continuing in this pattern can very well lead to having the lion feast on the very flesh I refuse to lay on the altar of the cross.

God has very harsh words for rebellion, comparing it to witchcraft. First Samuel 15:23 records the Lord's words to Saul through the prophet Samuel: "For rebellion is like the sin of divination, and defiance is like wickedness and idolatry. Because you have rejected the word of the LORD, He has rejected you as king."

The story of Saul is a cautionary one. Centuries before Christ, Saul was chosen to be the first king of Israel and was anointed by Samuel. God had commanded Saul to utterly destroy the Amalekite tribe. He was to spare nothing and no one. His army went to battle and soundly defeated the enemy. But Saul elevated his own reasoning above the Word of God, and he and his men spared the best of the sheep and oxen along with King Agag and all that was good in their eyes.

The Lord came to Samuel and told him that He regretted making Saul king. At first glance, it may appear that His regret was based on what Saul did. But God's regret was based on Saul's heart. When Samuel came to give Saul the Word of the Lord, he found that Saul had erected not an altar to the Lord but a monument to himself! (1 Sam. 15:12).

Saul said to Samuel, "May the LORD bless you. I have carried out the LORD's instructions" (v. 13). When Samuel confronted him with his disobedience, Saul protested, "But the people took some of the spoil, sheep and oxen, the choicest of the things devoted to destruction, to sacrifice to the LORD your God at Gilgal" (v. 21 NASB).

Not only did Saul blame the people, but he said they had spared the best to offer as sacrifices to the Lord. Samuel countered this reasoning, saying, "Does the LORD take pleasure in burnt offerings and sacrifices as much as in obeying the LORD? Look: to obey is better than sacrifice, to pay attention [is better] than the fat of rams" (v. 22 HCSB). In other words, God wants your obedience!

Saul had listened to the voice of the enemy and his flesh, which said, "No, you don't have to completely destroy it. After all, you can spare the best. Bring them back and offer them as sacrifices; God will like that." Have you heard similar lies in your own ear? "That's not what that Scripture really means" or "God will understand . . . you know He wants you to be happy."

As a result of Saul's pride, the kingdom was taken away and young David was anointed. The Lord chose David, the least and the youngest, because "God sees not as man sees, for man looks at the outward appearance, but the LORD looks at the heart" (1 Sam. 16:7 NASB).

Saul became jealous of David after the young shepherd's defeat of Goliath. Saul's proud heart led to his own torment. He tried to destroy David, but God's hand was on David and He protected him. Eventually Saul and his son, Jonathan, were killed in battle with the Philistines. David held no lingering grudge against his old rival, and he mourned over the losses of the former king and of his dear friend Jonathan. If you know about Jesus's lineage, you know how much God blessed that humility—David's bloodline would lead all the way to the Messiah.

Pride will do to us what it did to Saul if we don't repent. Our puffed up hearts will lead us to self-destruct. Many times I have counseled with women who have gone their own way. Much like Saul or the prodigal son, they usually don't recognize their pride and its deception until they have suffered much and sometimes lost everything. By the time they come to the end of themselves, there have been so many destructive consequences to their choices that the enemy has a tremendous hold over them.

As I have heard story after story, it has become easier for me to identify the place where that first door is opened to sin. Almost every time it is pride. Remember the magazine covers? *"Treat Yourself Right—You Deserve It." "Smart Ways to Get What You Really Want."* Or here's another one: *"A Happy Marriage? I'm Worth It!"*

Perhaps the prime testing ground for letting go of pride for women is in our marriages. The Lord has commanded us to submit to our husbands. The Amplified Bible's version of Ephesians 5:33 elaborates on what this means: "However, let each man of you [without exception] love his wife as [being in a sense] his very own self; and let the wife see that she respects and reverences her husband (that she notices him, regards him, honors him, prefers him, venerates him, and esteems him; and that she defers to him, praises him, and loves and admires him exceedingly)."

How many of us can say that we live up to that standard? The only way to honor and respect our husbands is to first submit to God. It's easy to point to the first part of that passage and say, "Well, I'll submit when he acts like the husband God commands him to be." But the truth is, we cannot be responsible for the behavior of another person. We must subdue our wills and do what God commands. Paul exhorts us to submit to our husbands as unto the Lord. When I submit to my husband, I am ultimately telling the Lord that I trust Him enough to submit. And guess where that submission leads? You know the answer by now: to the end of ourselves—to life in the Spirit—to More.

If you have felt the nudging of the Holy Spirit as you have read this chapter, you may want to pray and ask the Lord to enable you to conquer pride in the name of Jesus.

You may want to pray a prayer something like this:

Dear Heavenly Father,

You have revealed to me the pride and rebellion in my own heart. Lord, I choose to submit my life to You and to Your Word. I will deny myself, take up my cross daily, and follow You (Luke 9:23). May You be glorified in my life.

In Jesus name, Amen.

14

The Downward Spiral

For God has not given us a spirit of fear,
but of power and of love and of a sound mind.
2 TIMOTHY 1:7 (NKJV)

The passengers boarding the flight from London to Los Angeles were cautious, but everyone began to relax after takeoff. In mid-flight over Canada, a flight attendant noticed a suspicious object behind a seat and called the cockpit. The passengers got wind of her concern and panic spread like wildfire. The plane made an emergency landing in Edmonton, Alberta. The passengers were evacuated, and a bomb squad immediately began its work. The suspicious item? A cell phone. So goes the post 9/11 world where fear seems to be ever present.

When we allow pride and rebellion into our lives, we will many times also become victims of fear. Fear is one of Satan's primary tactics. It is based on lies from our flesh or the enemy. Consequently, fear isn't based on reality but on *assumed* reality. Many have said that the serpent's two fangs are fear and discouragement. He loves to intimidate us.

Scripture tells us we are to stand firm against the schemes of the enemy. We must face our fears. Second Timothy 1:7 says, "For God has not given a spirit of timidity [fear], but of power and love and discipline [sound mind]" (NASB). If God has not given it to us, then it is not of God, and we need to stand against it. I have heard it said that there are 365 "do not fears" in the Bible. I have never counted, but there are certainly a lot of them.

What are some of the things we fear? Terrorism, of course, is a threat we all live with post 9/11. Many people fear the economy. They are afraid of what will happen to the stock market, their investments, and their retirement. Some people have a fear of heights, of water, of spiders, of germs, even of crowds. Sometimes fears can become obsessive, turning into phobias.

The verb *to fear* has two somewhat different meanings, according to *Webster's*. The first is "to be afraid of." It suggests a state that can either be temporary or permanent (these days, it often seems to be a permanent way of life for many people).

The truth is that we do *not* need to fear in the sense of being frightened because the Lord is our refuge. Jesus Himself told His disciples words that we, too, can take to heart: "Peace I leave with you; My peace I give to you; not as the world gives do I give to you. Do not let your heart be troubled, nor let it be fearful" (John 14:27 NASB). He is our safe place. He is our stronghold.

Being in Awe of God Is Both Healthy and Essential

There is another definition of *to fear*, and that is the one we must be concerned with: "to have a reverential awe of." This kind of fear when applied to the Lord is not only a healthy response—

it is the only valid response. And it leads to the life that promises the More that is out there ready to be grasped:

- "The fear of the Lord is the beginning of wisdom" (Prov. 9:10).
- "To those who fear Him there is no want" (Ps. 34:9 NASB).
- The fear of the Lord is clean and endures forever (see Ps. 19:9).
- "The fear of the Lord prolongs life" (Prov. 10:27 NASB).
- The fear of the Lord leads to God's favor (see Ps. 147:11).
- The fear of the Lord keeps one away from evil (see Prov. 16:6).
- "The fear of the LORD is a fountain of life" (Prov. 14:27 NASB).
- "In the fear of the Lord one has strong confidence and his children have a refuge" (Prov. 14:26 NASB).

When your confidence is in the Lord, you will be filled with boldness. There is an inner awareness that you are covered and secure as long as you are in the center of your Father's will. He will guide and guard you. Do not be afraid!

In Matthew 10:28–31, Jesus said, "Don't fear [be frightened of] those who kill the body but are not able to kill the soul; rather, fear [be in awe of] Him who is able to destroy both soul and body in hell. Aren't two sparrows sold for a penny? Yet not one of them falls to the ground without your Father's consent. But even the hairs of your head have all been counted. Don't be afraid therefore; you are worth more than many sparrows." Our Abba loves us and knows us so intimately that He could tally up the very number of hairs on our heads. Not only is He aware; He also is in control of our lives. We can trust Him because He will take care of us.

As I write this chapter, my family has just returned from our first "Journeys of Paul" trip. We toured many of the places Paul visited in Turkey and Greece, with our tour ending in Rome. We visited Rome's Marmitime Prison and the Church of St. Paul at the Three Fountains, built over the traditional place of Paul's martyrdom. Behind the central fountain in the church is a recessed room with a beautiful painting that stretches from the floor to the ceiling. It depicts Paul's decapitated body with the Roman soldier, sword in hand, standing over him. The crowd in the painting responded—some in horror, others with indifference. But my eye was drawn to the top of the painting where Paul was being taken into heaven by angels and was being welcomed by the Lord. A dove was above him, with light radiating out and spilling onto Paul. His countenance was full of joy! Tears spilled down my upturned face and my own heart was filled with joy as I witnessed this example of "No fear!"

Knowing Our Abba Is the Antidote to Fear

Romans 8:15 says, "For you have not received a spirit of slavery leading to fear again, but you have received a spirit of adoption as sons by which we cry out, 'Abba! Father!'" (NASB). Our Abba, our "Dad," hears our cries, and we do not need to be afraid.

On my husband Steve's first trip to the Holy Land, he was having dinner in his hotel on the eve of the Sabbath. There were several Jewish families there having dinner as well. As he stood at the buffet table preparing his plate, he heard a little girl in a high chair calling out to her father. She cried, "Abba! Abba!" Her father replied to her in Hebrew. He readily responded to her when she called him by that name. What a beautiful picture of our relationship with our own Abba!

First John 4:18 is an antidote for fear: "There is no fear in love, but perfect love casts out fear, because fear involves punishment, and the one who fears is not perfected [mature] in love" (NASB). We have the love of our Abba, who will readily respond with love, not with punishment, when we call out to Him.

To be *perfected* means "to be mature." When we were children, we had many childish fears. You may remember being afraid that there was something or someone under your bed at night. If you were like me, you would get a running start at the door of your room and jump onto your bed to keep your foot from being grabbed. Silly fears for those of us who are adults, and yet for a child they feel very real. So it is with our relationship with the Lord. As we mature in our faith, we understand more fully our Abba's faithfulness, and His great love dispels *all* our fears.

Refusing to face our fears and instead giving in to them can begin the downward spiral that leads to depression. In *Praying God's Word,* Beth Moore describes the way most people characterize depression: "Ongoing depression becomes a stronghold because its very nature is to eclipse a sense of well-being and hopefulness, strangling abundant life. Ask ten people to describe their depression with one word only and overwhelmingly the common response will be 'darkness'" (250).

For many, depression is comparable to a dark hole, a pit, or a dungeon. It is in this dark place that we feel isolated, lonely, discouraged, hopeless, and overwhelmed. The mundane duties of life are suddenly too difficult to accomplish.

I have always been an extremely optimistic person. I was raised in a home that was very positive. But after the birth of our fourth child, I experienced what I now know was a mild case of depression. My two oldest children were in school. Our son was playing baseball and the two older girls, ages six and three, were taking ballet. I was in charge of a large women's conference that we had scheduled the year before. One of my dear friends who helped with our women's ministry was battling metastasized breast cancer. Life caved in on me.

I was physically and emotionally exhausted. I felt so tired and drained! I remember walking into my laundry room and just turning around and walking back out. I couldn't face the laundry or a sink full of dirty dishes. When we are depressed, everything *feels* overwhelming. But we must understand that it is a *feeling*— it is not reality. By the grace of God and the power of His Word, He pulled me through this dark time in my life.

Obviously there are very real emotional and physical causes for some cases of depression. That is why it is so important to see your doctor if you are experiencing any of the symptoms of depression. If you have a chemical imbalance in your body, take the medication prescribed by your doctor. There may even be times when you go through a temporary bout of depression and medication can help pull you through until you can be weaned off the medicine under the care of your physician. Whether your depression is rooted in physical or emotional causes, the enemy will take advantage. He is the one who comes in and plants thoughts of hopelessness, despair, and possibly even suicide.

It is quite possible that the reason behind the accelerating numbers of people diagnosed with depression in our culture is that some people refuse to face and deal with their fears or the pain in their lives—they merely seek to dull or numb them through medication. Could it be that our culture's emphasis on "self" and on instant gratification has caused a lack of gratitude and thanksgiving that has led to an unhealthy preoccupation with self? Ask yourself if you have opened the door to the enemy through pride or rebellion, which has led to fear and has now spiraled out of control into depression.

While there is always a risk of oversimplifying the complex causes of depression, a preoccupation with self does lead to an ungrateful spirit. Paul instructs us, "Therefore as you have received Christ Jesus the Lord, so walk in Him, having been firmly rooted and now being built up in Him and established in your faith, just as you were instructed, and *overflowing with gratitude.* See to it that no one takes you captive through philosophy and empty deception, according to the tradition of men, according to the elementary principles of the world, rather than according to Christ" (Col. 2:6–8 NASB, emphasis mine). The *Expositor's Bible Commentary* states, "The present passage may imply that those who lack a deep sense of thankfulness to God are especially vulnerable to doubt and spiritual delusion" (vol. 11, 196). As you examine yourself, do you detect a lack of gratitude that has caused you to doubt God's Word?

God's Word Is the Key
That Unlocks the Dungeons of Despair and Doubt

Do not give in to despair! Stand against it as you stand on the Word of God. Madame Guyon has said, "I implore you to not give in to despair. It is a dangerous temptation, because our Adversary has refined it to the point that it is quite subtle. Hopelessness constricts and withers the heart, rendering it unable to sense God's blessings and grace. It also causes you to exaggerate the adversities of life and makes your burdens seem too heavy for you to bear. Yet God's plans for you and His ways of bringing about His plans are infinitely wise" (as quoted in Cowman, *Streams in the Desert,* 217).

It may be time to remember that God has given us the key to our dungeon. It is the same key described in John Bunyan's beloved classic *The Pilgrim's Progress.* The main character, Christian, is an allegorical picture of believers on their way to heaven. His spiritual journey on earth is chronicled for all who travel behind him.

After wandering off the path to the Celestial City, Christian finds himself thrown into the dungeon of Doubting Castle by Giant Despair. He and his companion Hopeful are dejected and fearful. All hope seems to have vanished:

> Well, on Saturday about midnight they began to pray and continued in prayer till almost break of day.
>
> Now, a little before it was Day, good Christian, as one half amazed, brake out in this passionate speech; What a Fool, quoth he, am I, thus to lie in a stinking dungeon, when I may as well walk at liberty? I have a key in my boson, called Promise, that will I am persuaded open any lock in Doubting-Castle. Then said Hopeful, That's good news, good brother, pluck it out of thy bosom and try. (106–107)[1]

---

1. Spellings, capitalization, and punctuation have been retained from the early versions of this Christian classic, which was first published in 1678.

God's Word is the key that not only opens the door of the dungeon but every door in Doubting Castle. After they escape and are back up on the King's Highway, Christian and Hopeful erect a pillar with a warning for all who would come behind them.

It is interesting to note that John Bunyan wrote *The Pilgrim's Progress* while in jail, where he was imprisoned for twelve years. During the long passages of day upon day, month upon month, his body was behind bars but his soul was free. He penned a work of hope in God's faithfulness that is the very antithesis of despair.

Regardless of how you end up in your own dungeon—by wrong choices or by the circumstances of this fallen world—the way out is the same. We must do as Christian did and use the Word of God to infuse hope back into our battle-weary souls.

Our God said, "Let there be light," and He can still bring His light and glory into our darkness. He has given us His precious promises, and just as Christian used them to open the door of his dungeon, God's Word can and will set us free as well. But we must use the key. We can't just carry it with us. It is our sword of offense against the enemy. We must practice sword-wielding.

Ask the Lord to give you specific promises to use against the temptations to fear and despair that the enemy hurls against you. It is through the Word of God that we poke holes in the foundation that supports the strongholds of the enemy. Confess fear and discouragement. "Submit therefore to God. Resist the devil and he will flee from you" (James 4:7 NASB). *The Message* puts it this way: "So let God work his will in you. Yell a loud *no* to the devil and watch him scamper. Say a quick *yes* to God and He'll be there in no time."

Sometimes the way out is almost instantaneous, but other times it is a long climb to the light in the distance. Don't just seek the way out: seek Christ in the midst of your darkness. As you strengthen yourself with His Word and long to know Him more intimately, He will reveal Himself. "You will seek Me and find Me when you search for Me with all your heart" (Jer. 29:13). We must long for Him more than we long for relief. As the Lord told Abraham, "Do not be afraid, Abram. I am your shield, your very great reward" (Gen. 15:1 NIV).

Take a moment and ask the Lord to enable you to face your fears. Confess the discouraging thoughts that have bombarded your mind. Be still before Him. You may want to pray a prayer something like this:

Dear Heavenly Father,

I know that you have not given me a spirit of fear. Therefore, I refuse to fear or to be anxious. Instead, I will pray with thanksgiving and let my requests be made known to You. I thank You that Your peace, which passes all comprehension, will guard my heart and my mind. Father, I confess that I have feared _____ _____. Please forgive me. I choose to place my trust in You and keep my eyes on Jesus! Please help me to take every thought captive to the obedience of Christ. May I glorify You as I place my faith in You and You alone![2]

In Jesus's name, Amen.

---

2. 2 Tim. 1:7 and Phil. 4:6–7 are source material for this prayer.

15

The Power of the Spoken Word
(Part 1)

For the word of God is living and active and sharper
than any two-edged sword, and piercing as far as the division
of soul and spirit, of both joints and marrow, and able
to judge the thoughts and intentions of the heart.
HEBREWS 4:12 (NASB)

*I*n his most well-known Narnia chronicle, *The Lion, the Witch and the Wardrobe*, C. S. Lewis weaves a fascinating tale of adventure and fantasy that records the journey of four children—Peter, Susan, Edmund, and Lucy—throughout the land of Narnia. Early on, Edmund becomes enchanted with the evil White Witch, who has cast a spell on Narnia making it "always winter but never Christmas." Edmund sneaks away from the other children to join the witch and her wicked companions.

The three remaining children meet Mr. and Mrs. Beaver, who agree to take them to see Aslan, the lion. The Beavers explain that

Aslan alone has the power to break the spell of the White Witch and save Edmund. On their journey they meet Father Christmas, who explains that Christmas has finally arrived and that the witch's power is growing weaker. Father Christmas then gives the children presents. "They are tools and not toys," he explains. "The time to use them is perhaps near at hand. Bear them well."

> With these words he handed to Peter a shield and a sword. The shield was the colour of silver and across it there ramped a red lion, as bright as a red strawberry at the moment when you pick it. The hilt of the sword was of gold and it had a sheath and a sword belt and everything it needed, and it was just the right size and weight for Peter to use. Peter was silent and solemn as he received these gifts for he felt that they were a very serious kind of present. (104)

And indeed, they were very serious gifts. Peter wielded his sword to kill the White Witch's captain, Fenris Ulf, in the battle for Narnia.

We, too, are engaged in a grave battle against the forces of darkness that seek to destroy us. Perhaps the first thing we should see each morning is a sign that reads: *You are now entering the battlefield—weapons required.* The Sword of the Spirit, God's Word, will give us the winning edge over our evil opponent. Speaking the Word of God is how we wield our swords. There is tremendous power in the spoken Word.

With His Spoken Word, God Created the World

Genesis 1:3 states, "God said, 'Let there be light,' and there was light." God spoke, and everything we know and experience

146

in our world was created. Follow the verses throughout the chapter and over and over again you read "God said." Verse 26 records the creation of man when God said, "Let Us make man in Our image, according to Our likeness."

Genesis 2:7 tells us that God made "man of the dust of the ground, and breathed into his nostrils the breath of life; and man became a living being" (NKJV). We are living beings who were created to bear the image of our Father. But we recognize that because of sin we are marred image bearers. Because of Jesus Christ and His Spirit who lives within us once we are saved, we are again capable of bearing His image to a lost world.

The Father, Son, and Spirit are the "Us" in whose image we were created. John 1:1–3 and 1:14 tell us: "In the beginning was the Word, and the Word was with God, and the Word was God. He was in the beginning with God. All things came into being by Him, and apart from Him nothing came into being that has come into being. . . . And the Word became flesh, and dwelt among us, and we beheld His glory, glory as of the only begotten from the Father, full of grace and truth" (NASB).

Here's the remarkable fact about this statement: This living Word of God is our Savior, Jesus! He put on skin and came to this earth through the womb of a virgin. He became one of us, that He might take our place: in life—living sinless; in death—paying our debt. Now that's what I call power in God's Word!

Through His Spoken Word God Will Consummate the End of Time

In Revelation 19 we see that just as God through His Word created everything that we know, God through His Word will consummate the end of time. The Living Word, Jesus, will return as King of kings and Lord of lords, destroying the enemy with His Word.

Scripture tells us that our words are important too. We will actually be judged by our words. In Matthew 12:34–37 Jesus said to the Pharisees, "You brood of vipers, how can you, being evil, speak what is good? For the mouth speaks out of that which fills the heart. The good man brings out of his good treasure what is good; and the evil man brings out of his evil treasure what is evil. But I tell you that every careless word that people speak, they shall give an accounting for it in the day of judgment. For by your words you will be justified and by your words you will be condemned" (NASB).

When we asked Christ to come into our lives, He set us apart. We are now to be representatives of the living Word of God to this lost world. Consequently, we will be held accountable for our words because there is tremendous power to impart life or to bring death and destruction through our tongues. Scripture is very clear that what fills our hearts, which is what we think about and dwell on, will come out of our mouths. That is who we really are.

When people suffer from fear or anxiety, they are focusing on what they fear. The fear begins to loom larger and larger until it eclipses our solution, who is our Savior. We must set our minds on Christ and on the things that are above (Col. 3:1), and we must fill our minds with the Word of God on our subject, whatever it may be.

How do we do that? By searching the Scriptures so that we know what that Word is and then meditating and praying on what we have found. Then we are able to take our fearful or anxious thoughts captive to the obedience of Christ and replace the lies of the enemy with the truth of God's Word. It is only when we actively engage with the spoken Word of God, as Jesus did when He was tempted by Satan in the wilderness, that we will have victory.

Through His Word God Fulfills What He Says He Will Do

God's Word strengthens us in our inner person. His Word produces faith—"Faith comes from hearing, and hearing by the word of Christ" (Rom. 10:17 NASB). Then and only then are we able to "walk by faith, not by sight" (2 Cor. 5:7). With our eyes fixed on Jesus, He dispels our fears, enables us to forgive, and gives us the self-control we need to release anger and bitterness or anything else that has held us captive. Once our hearts are purified and no longer divided, we will bring forth life from His Spirit, who fills our inner person.

Scripture is replete with examples of the importance and seriousness of words. Numbers 12 gives us an example of how God dealt with rebellious words against His prophet Moses. Miriam and Aaron spoke against Moses and the Cushite woman whom he had married: "Does the LORD speak only through Moses? Does He not also speak through us?" (v. 2). Their words implied that they felt just as important as Moses. After all, they were the older brother and sister. Who did he think he was, anyway? Their spoken words revealed not only their rebellion but also the jealousy in their hearts. The Bible says, "The LORD heard it" (v. 2 NASB).

God called all three of them out of the tent of meeting. He came to them in a pillar of cloud and set them straight: "If there is a prophet among you from the LORD, I make Myself known to him in a vision; I speak with him in a dream. Not so with My servant Moses; he is faithful in all My household. I speak with him directly, openly, and not in riddles; he sees the form of the LORD. So why were you not afraid to speak against My servant Moses?" (vv. 6–8).

The anger of the Lord burned against them and His presence departed. When all was calm again, Miriam was white with leprosy. Moses cried out to the Lord on her behalf. The Lord told him that she would be shut up outside the camp for seven days, and then she would be restored. But in the meantime everyone would see her reproach. I would say that the Lord took their words very seriously!

What about the Israelite spies? Their story is recorded in Numbers 13 and 14. God told the spies to go into the land of Canaan and see how wonderful it was and then come back and tell the people. Ten of the spies allowed fear to fill their hearts, and they came back with a negative report. They said, "The cities are fortified and the people are like giants. We felt like grasshoppers in their sight."

Their fear instilled fear into the hearts of the other Israelites. The people began to complain against Moses. Only Joshua and Caleb had God's perspective. They said the land was great! They believed God had removed His protection from those people, and He was giving the land into the Israelites' hands. All they had to do was to go in and possess it.

But the Israelite people's fear led to unbelief. In fact, God punished them for it. They had cried out saying they wished they had died in Egypt. They feared for their children's lives if they entered this new land. So God sentenced them to forty years in the wilderness, one year for every day that the spies had spent in Canaan. In fact, God told the priest Aaron to say to them:

As surely as I live, *declares* the LORD, I will do to
you exactly as I heard you *say*. Your corpses will fall in
this wilderness—all of you who were registered [in the
census], the entire number of you 20 years old or more—
because you have *complained* about Me. I *swear* that none
of you will enter the land I promised to settle you in,
except Caleb son of Jephunneh and Joshua son of Nun.
I will bring your children whom you *said* would become
plunder into the land you rejected, and they will enjoy
it. But as for you, your corpses will fall in this wilderness.
Your children will be shepherds in the wilderness for 40
years and bear the penalty for your acts of unfaithfulness
until all your corpses lie [scattered] in the wilderness. You
will bear the consequences of your sins 40 years based
on the number of the 40 days that you scouted the land,
a year for each day. You will know My displeasure. I, the
LORD, *have spoken. I swear* that I will do this to the entire
evil community that has *conspired* against Me. They will
come to an end in the wilderness, and there they will die.
(Num. 14:28–35, emphases mine)

The ten spies who had given the negative report died of a
plague, but God spared and blessed Caleb and Joshua. Did you
notice that the Lord said to them that it would be done to them
exactly as they had spoken? After all the plagues and miracles
they had experienced, how could the Israelites doubt the Word
of the Lord?

We must ask ourselves that same question: How can we who
know that God the Father sent His only Son clothed in flesh to
walk in this sin-infested world, to willingly lay down His life for

us—to die, be buried, and to be raised back to life—not believe? Not only has He saved us, but He has also sent His Spirit to dwell within us, making us living, breathing temples of our God. We are His children. How can we who have experienced forgiveness, who have experienced the filling of the Holy Spirit, not believe?

Did you notice the response of Moses, the man God called "a very humble man, more so than any man on the face of the earth" (Num. 12:3)? Every time the people rebelled, Moses would fall on his face before the Lord and intercede for them. Many times he would pray God's own words back to Him.

In Numbers 14:20, after Moses' intercession, God said, "I have pardoned them according to your word" (NASB). The power of the Word of God—and the words of a righteous person—are awesome!

When we harbor rebellion and unbelief in our hearts, we will doubt God and His Word, and the lack of belief comes out in our own words. In Moses' day the majority of the people believed the bad report. What does this tell us about the majority? The majority of people, even Christian people, live life by what they can see with their physical eyes. We must first surrender to the Lord so that He can open our Spirit eyes and allow us to see all that God has planned and prepared for us. There may be a promised land of blessings lying just before us. What do we miss because of unbelief?

In the next chapter we will apply the truths of the power of your own spoken words. How are your words affecting your life? Ask God to prepare you for this essential issue.

16

The Power
of the Spoken Word
(Part 2)

He who guards his lips guards his life.
PROVERBS 13:3 NIV

*I*t has been well said, "By examining the tongue of the patient, physicians find out the diseases of the body, and philosophers the diseases of the mind." By listening to someone talk, you will know what is in his or her heart. You will know in whom that person trusts. You won't have to listen long to make that determination. It will be very evident.

As Christians, our speech should reflect the fact that we belong to Jesus Christ. In Ephesians 4:23 Paul exhorts us to be "renewed in the spirit of [our] mind." Our thoughts will determine our speech. *The Message* states Ephesians 4:29–32 in these modern terms: "Watch the way you talk. Let nothing foul or dirty come out of your mouth. Say only what helps, each word a gift. Don't grieve God. Don't break his heart. His Holy Spirit, moving and breathing in you, is the most intimate part of your life, making you fit for himself. Don't take such a gift for granted. Make a clean break with all cutting, backbiting, profane talk. Be gentle with one another, sensitive. Forgive one another as quickly and thoroughly as God in Christ forgave you."

The verse on grieving the Spirit is in the context of verses that talk about the tongue. We are only to speak those words that edify or build up. Remember those new garments we are to put on? When we put on the new self, it will be revealed in our speech.

You may be thinking that there are times when confrontation or correction needs to take place. Yes, sometimes it does, but the truth must be spoken in love. We never speak to inflict pain but to encourage Christlikeness. In Matthew 15:18–19, Jesus reminds us of the kind of speech that will come out of our mouths if we speak as we did before we put on our new self: "But what comes out of the mouth comes from the heart, and this defiles a man. For from the heart come evil thoughts, murders, adulteries, sexual immoralities, thefts, false testimonies, blasphemies."

If we reflect back on the twelve Israeli spies sent to scout out the Promised Land, we see an example of God's response to the spies' reports that illustrates the power of words. Only two of the twelve, Joshua and Caleb, saw the potential of the land. The other ten gave reports filled with negativity—"The people living in the land are strong, and the cities are large and fortified" (Num. 13:28). But notice Caleb's report: "We must go up and take possession of the land because we can certainly conquer it!" (v. 30).

Those who believed the negative report and doubted God suffered for their unbelief. The census of the people taken at Mt. Sinai reported in Numbers 1 states that there were 603,550 males aged twenty or older. Only the tribe of Levi was not counted in the census. If there were as many women as men of this age, that means more than one million people died in the wilderness and only two of that age group actually entered the Promised Land: Joshua and Caleb.

God blessed and sustained Caleb for his faithfulness. Caleb was just as strong at eighty-five years of age as he had been at forty. God honored Caleb because he followed Him with "his whole heart." God gave him the ability to see with Spirit eyes. He knew God had called His people into the Promised Land and would be faithful to take them in.

When we trust God completely, He enables us to discern good from evil. Scripture tells us: "Solid food is for the mature—for those whose senses have been trained to distinguish between good and evil" (Heb. 5:14). With this discernment, the Spirit will warn us before we speak evil. How do we know when we are about to speak something that shouldn't come out of our mouths? We need to ask if it will edify. Will it bring grace to those who hear? Many times the Spirit Himself will warn us with what some call "the quickening of the Spirit"—another description is "that still small voice." At that split second we have a choice to make. We can either choose to speak it anyway, or we can bite our tongues and say nothing.

Out of the Heart the Mouth Speaks

We must choose to allow only wholesome words to proceed out of our mouths. That choice is an act of the will. It will become less difficult as we continually fill our minds with those things that are good. Paul tells us: "Finally, brethren, whatever is true, whatever is honorable, whatever is right, whatever is pure, whatever is lovely, whatever is of good repute, if there is any excellence and if anything worthy of praise, dwell on these things" (Phil. 4:8 NASB).

When I was a teenager, I had a pretty sharp tongue. I was strong willed and could be rebellious, especially in my speech. I have apologized to my mother over and over for how difficult I was to raise. I'm sure my parents developed calluses on their knees before I left home for college. Did you know there is a warning in Proverbs about a sharp tongue? "There is one who speaks rashly like the thrusts of a sword, but the tongue of the wise brings healing" (Prov. 12:18 NASB).

We must be especially careful about sarcasm. Sometimes it seems harmless to jab at someone with sarcastic humor. But we should never get a laugh at someone else's expense. Paul warns us about "coarse jesting" in Ephesians 5:4 (NASB).

In fact, we don't even need to make fun of ourselves. *We will never rise above who we believe we are.* If we condemn ourselves, we will be more likely to entertain the condemning thoughts of the enemy. When he shoots us with the flaming arrows of fear, inadequacy, rejection, unbelief, and a host of other arrows, we will fall prey to his assault.

Let us take to heart what God says about us. Remember Andrew Murray's definition of humility? "The humble person is not one who thinks meanly of himself; he simply doesn't think of himself at all." Instead, let us make much of God and His glory. If our eyes are fixed on Jesus, we won't be such an easy target for Satan's arrows.

The enemy hits women hard with feelings of inadequacy. We are continually comparing ourselves with others or with the women we see on television or on magazine covers. We must get beyond these feelings by making the most of who God has created us to be and then focusing on what He has called us to do while we are on earth. If we will focus on loving and reaching out to others, we won't be paranoid about our own shortcomings. It isn't about us, anyway. This life is about Jesus!

If We Think Like Christ, Our Words Will Reflect Our Thoughts

I challenge you to do something. The next time you walk into a room of people, ask the Lord who He wants you to encourage. You are His ambassador and His representative. Our citizenship is in heaven; we are simply representing our King in the time that He gives us on this earth. Every encounter can be a divine appointment.

Our Father is equipping us to take every thought captive to the obedience of Jesus Christ. We must take prisoner every debilitating and condemning thought. It is only then that we are able to replace the lie with the truth of God's Word. When you think right (like Christ), you will act right (like Christ).

James 3 has some very strong words about the tongue. He tells us if we can discipline our tongues, we can discipline our whole bodies. The tongue may be one of the smallest members of the body, yet it is the most difficult to control. In verse 6 he says, "And the tongue is a flame of fire. It is a whole world of wickedness, corrupting your entire body. It can set your whole life on fire, for it is set on fire by hell itself" (NLT). Our tongues can destroy the good plan God has for us because we won't rise above what we speak, which reveals what we believe. He is telling us we will be justified by our words and we will be condemned by our words. It is surely true that we don't realize the power and impact of what we say.

Even though our words are powerful, we can't just speak and claim anything we desire by tacking on "in Jesus's name." I am not part of the "name it and claim it" group. But our God has given us His precious promises, and He expects us to appropriate them to experience the abundant life—a life of More. Are we experiencing it? Or are we allowing negative thoughts and doubts from the enemy, which are expressed in words, to steal what is rightfully ours and make us satisfied with less? When we choose to think and speak God's Word, we are wielding the Sword of the Spirit. The very weapon that Jesus used against the enemy is ours as well.

We must think and speak in faith. The book of Hebrews tells us, "Faith is the assurance of things hoped for, the conviction of things not seen," and "without faith it is impossible to please Him" (Heb. 11:1, 6 NASB). We must take God at His Word. That means adjusting our lives and our thoughts—and our words—to match His truth.

The Old Testament book of Proverbs is full of instructions and admonitions about the tongue:

- "The one who guards his mouth preserves his life; the one who opens wide his lips comes to ruin" (13:3 NASB).
- "Gentle words are a tree of life; a deceitful tongue crushes the spirit" (15:4 NLT).
- "Everyone enjoys a fitting reply; it is wonderful to say the right thing at the right time!" (15:23 NLT).
- "The heart of the wise instructs his mouth and adds persuasiveness to his lips" (16:23 NASB).

- "Death and life are in the power of the tongue, and those who love it will eat its fruit" (18:21 NASB).

Scripture also warns us about specific sinful kinds of speech:

- excessive talking (Prov. 10:19, 18:7)
- careless words (Matt. 12:36–37)
- gossip (Lev. 19:16; Prov. 18:8, 20:19)
- lies (Prov. 6:16–19, 12:22; John 8:44)
- flattery (Ps. 12:1–3; Prov. 2:16, 7:21)
- sarcasm (Ps. 64:3)
- criticism and complaints (Eph. 4:29–30).

If We Speak Words of Blessing to Others, We'll Impart God's Grace and Life to Them

Don't you want to be an imparter of life? Our words should be words of grace and life. Proverbs 11:16 says, "A gracious woman attains honor" (NASB). Our words need to be words of blessing. We need to speak blessings into the lives of our family members and into the lives of our friends and associates. People are drawn to those who impart life.

What about your children? Are you praying for them and asking the Lord to give you wisdom as you train them according to His plan for their lives? Do you speak words that encourage them to pursue their areas of strength and giftedness? Do you see who God has created them to be? Do you speak blessings over them? You can do this using actual Scripture promises. (For examples of how to speak blessings, I recommend *Bless Your Children Every Day* by Dr. Mary Ruth Swope, *The Gift of the*

Blessing by Gary Smalley and John Trent, and *Blessing Your Spirit* by Sylvia Gunter and Arthur Burk—I've added publishing information in the bibliography so you can more easily locate copies.) As you speak what the Lord is revealing to you, it will resonate in your children's own spirits. Something will ring true about your words, and they will desire to rise to the bright future that you are verbalizing.

In Larry Crabb's book *Connecting: Healing Ourselves and Our Relationships,* he tells of a fifth-grade teacher who recognized Larry's ability with words. The teacher told him that he thought he could be a writer. Those words confirmed a stirring in Larry's soul and began the release of what God had intended for his life. He writes, "I wonder what more could be set in motion by visionary words from sensitive members of our community? What could parents say to their children, husbands to wives and wives to husbands, friends to friends, and shepherds to those entrusted to their care? 'Consider what a great forest is set on fire by a small spark' (James 3:5). That passage refers to the damage caused by evil words, but the reverse holds as well: Visionary words can release enormous good. 'The tongue has the power of life and death' (Prov. 18:21)" (159).

It's time to submit this small member of our body to the Lord for His glory. As we do, our words will become tools of edification and encouragement. "Therefore encourage one another and build up one another, just as you also are doing" (1 Thess. 5:11 NASB).

For our words to reflect Christ, we must begin with our thoughts. As our thoughts are taken captive to the obedience of Christ, our hearts are set free to run after Him, and we then ascend His holy hill with cleansed hands and purified hearts. Our hearts and minds will be transformed, and we will begin to speak life into those we love and touch.

I am closing this chapter with a blessing that you can speak out loud. This blessing is a confirmation of what the Word of God says about who you are. My prayer for you is that you will always have a reverent fear of the Lord and a respect for His Word. I bless you with faith to believe God and to take Him at His Word.

Blessing

I am fearfully and wonderfully made. In His book the days that were ordained for me were all written. How precious are His thoughts toward me! I am loved with an everlasting love by my Abba. He will never leave me or forsake me. He has called me by name to be His, a child of the King of the universe, a joint heir with Christ. I have been sealed with His Spirit, and nothing can by any means separate me from Him. He has a good plan for my life, and He has gifted me to fulfill His calling. I am an overcomer, more than a conqueror. He has given me authority over all the power of the enemy, and nothing will by any means harm me. No weapon formed against me will prosper, and I can do all things through Christ who strengthens me. He surrounds me with favor as a shield. I will rise up as a daughter of the King and claim my heritage as the woman of God that He has created me to be.[1]

---

1. Ps. 139; Jer. 31:3; Heb. 13:5; Rom. 8:17; Eph. 1:13; Rom. 8:38–39; Jer. 29:11; Luke 10:19; Isa. 54:17; Phil. 4:13; and Ps. 5:12 provide source material for this blessing.

17

The Lure of the Supernatural

Do not let your people practice fortune-telling,
or use sorcery, or interpret omens, or engage in witchcraft,
or cast spells, or function as mediums or psychics,
or call forth the spirits of the dead.
Anyone who does these things is detestable to the Lord.
DEUTERONOMY 18:10b–12a (NLT)

As spirit beings, we are always searching for a spiritual connection. Apart from Christ, people look in all the wrong places. Participation and study in the occult, Satanism, witchcraft, and the New Age movement, as well as other practices and belief systems, have grown at a disturbing rate in recent years. Barna research on teenage views about the supernatural from January 2006 revealed some alarming statistics: More than four out of five teenagers said they had witnessed supernatural themes in media in the last three months.

And they were not only observers—"Three-quarters of America's youth (73 percent) had engaged in at least one type of psychic or witchcraft-related activity, beyond mere media exposure or horoscope usage. The most common types of witchcraft behaviors were using an Ouija board and reading a book about witchcraft or Wicca, each of which had been done by more than one-third of teenagers. As for psychic activities, more than one-fourth of teens have had their palm read (30 percent) or their fortune told (27 percent)."

God's Word has some specific things to say about the occult. Deuteronomy 18:9–14 offers these instructions: "When you enter the land which the LORD your God gives you, you shall not learn to imitate the detestable things of those nations. There shall not be found among you anyone who makes his son or his daughter pass through the fire, one who uses divination, one who practices witchcraft, or one who interprets omens, or a sorcerer, or one who casts a spell or a medium, or a spiritist, or one who calls up the dead. For whoever does these things is detestable to the LORD; and because of these detestable things the LORD your God will drive them out before you. You shall be blameless before the LORD your God" (NASB).

The Lord is clear—we are to have nothing to do with anything demonic or anything resembling it. These things are "detestable"—there could hardly be a stronger adjective to describe His feelings about occult activity. We are not to allow our sons or daughters, or by extension anyone in our care or in our household, to participate in them.

Our youngest daughter was in the third grade when the Harry Potter books first became popular. She wanted to see the first movie that was about to be shown in our city. I sat down with her and asked her to read the passage out of Deuteronomy 18.

After reading what the Lord said about sorcery, she no longer had a desire to see the movie or to read the books.

I realize there are some Christians who may not see a problem with similar children's books. Your decision is between you and the Lord. But I urge you and caution you not to allow anything to come into your home or into your children's tender minds that the enemy can use to erect a stronghold.

Take Authority Over Evil Influences on Your Home and Family

As a parent, you have an obligation and responsibility, along with the authority, to protect your home and family from evil influences. You have a right to demand that nothing demonic or of the occult be brought into it. Nothing that displeases the Lord or that He detests should be allowed to come in and defile it. Resolve to be like Joshua, who said, "As for me and my house, we will serve the Lord."

The Old Testament gives further instructions to God's people about these practices. Leviticus 19:31 says, "Do not turn to mediums or spiritists; do not seek them out to be defiled by them. I am the LORD your God" (NASB). Then in Leviticus 20:6–8, God says, "As for the person who turns to mediums and to spiritists, to play the harlot after them, I will also set My face against that person and will cut him off from among his people. You shall consecrate yourselves therefore and be holy, for I am the LORD your God. You shall keep My statutes and practice them; I am the LORD who sanctifies you" (NASB). God leaves no doubt about how He feels about witchcraft or anything that would honor

Satan or his demons. It should be detestable to us because it is detestable to Him.

In the New Testament, the book of Acts describes how early Christians handled witchcraft and sorcery. Paul was in Ephesus teaching and preaching in the synagogues. He taught there for two years, and all who lived in Asia heard the Word of the Lord and saw God perform extraordinary miracles at the hand of Paul. There were some Jewish exorcists, seven sons of a Jewish chief priest, who had heard Paul take authority over the enemy. Trying to imitate Paul, they said to a demonized man, "I command you in the name of Jesus, whom Paul preaches, to come out!" (Acts 19:13 NLT).

The evil spirit answered, "I recognize Jesus, and I know about Paul, but who are you?" (Acts 19:15 NASB). In other words, you have no authority over me; you don't belong to Jesus Christ. Scripture records what happened to these men: "The man, in whom was the evil spirit, leaped on them and subdued all of them and overpowered them, so that they fled out of that house naked and wounded. And this became known to all, both Jews and Greeks who lived in Ephesus; and fear fell upon them all and the name of the Lord Jesus was being magnified. Many also of those who had believed kept coming, confessing and disclosing their practices. And many of those who practiced magic brought their books together and began burning them in the sight of everyone; and they counted up the price of them and found it fifty thousand pieces of silver" (Acts 19:16–19 NASB).

The Spirit of God speaking through Paul led the people of Ephesus to bring all their books of sorcery and magic together, and they burned them all in a huge public bonfire. The books were worth fifty thousand pieces of silver! According to the John

MacArthur Study Bible, that was "fifty thousand days' wages for a common laborer—an astonishing sum of money given to indicate how widespread the practice of magic was in Ephesus" (1636). What a remarkable example! When God manifests His Spirit among His people, they will see themselves as they really are and will respond in repentance and obedience.

Discard Practices and Things in Your Home That Dishonor God

If there are any items in our homes that don't honor Christ, they need to be taken out. The psalmist in Psalm 101:2b–3 makes a promise to God that should be ours as well: "I will walk within my house in the integrity of my heart. I will set no worthless thing before my eyes; I hate the work of those who fall away; it shall not fasten its grip on me" (NASB). That means we need to take out any movies, posters, books, CDs, or anything else that would not please the Lord.

Do you remember going to slumber parties as a little girl? You may have participated in activities that you thought were harmless at the time. Did you ever take part in "Bloody Mary," asking questions of an Ouija board, automatic writing, interpreting tarot cards, blood pacts, "light as a feather," or other occult games? What about palm reading, horoscopes, or séances? Any of them can give the enemy a foothold in our lives. We must confess them, repent, and take back any ground we have given to the enemy.

We must all examine ourselves, pray, and ask for forgiveness for allowing any of these activities to compromise our walk with the Lord, and then stop the offending activity immediately and permanently.

You might pray a prayer like the one below:

Heavenly Father,
I desire to love You and follow You with a pure heart.
I confess my involvement in _____
(pray over each one individually). I ask You to forgive me,
and I take back the ground I had given to the enemy in
this area. I bow before Jesus Christ alone.
In Jesus's name, Amen.

18

Purity Begins Within

Do you not know that your body is a temple
of the Holy Spirit who is in you, whom you have from God,
and that you are not your own?
1 CORINTHIANS 6:19 (NASB)

Sex sells. You would have to have your head in a hole not to notice. It's on billboards and in commercials, newspaper ads, and magazines. Because we were created for relational intimacy, it is easy to fall prey to the lies and perversion of the enemy and believe that a physical relationship will satisfy our needs. When we allow the enemy to defraud us sexually, we will find not only that sex sells but that it will sell us out.

The Moriah House in Memphis is a part of the Memphis Union Mission and a refuge for women and children who need a place to live while they allow the Lord to put their lives back together. At a recent visit there, I heard one of the graduates of the ministry share her story of drugs, abuse, prostitution, abortion, and the adult entertainment industry. I was also awed by the power of the Lord to change a life. She is graduating from college and coming back to work with the women in this ministry. What a powerful testimony!

My daughters and I prepared "heritage books" for each of the residents of the Moriah House. A friend had started this tradition earlier by making one for me. I then made one for our oldest daughter, Lindsey, and our middle daughter, Alli, when they graduated from high school. The books consist of Scriptures and a letter to them declaring who they are in Christ and blessing them with the future the Lord has for them.

Each of the women's books contained a letter I had written to them. Most of them are first-generation Christians. They are now joint heirs with Christ and have a tremendous heritage of blessing to pass on to future generations. This is part of the letter:

Dear Sister in Christ,

I want you to know how much God loves you and desires to meet your deepest needs. Read and know the Word of God, for you will meet Him there. The Lord will continue to speak to you through His Word and also through the writings of others who have walked closely and deeply with Him. Don't ever lose the wonder of your relationship with Jesus! He is what life is all about. Allow Him to guide you, woo you, and wow you! Stay in His Word. There is nothing more powerful than the spoken Word of God. Know and use your Sword well!

In Christ, you have received a great treasure—a heritage of faith. I give you this heritage book in anticipation of how the Lord will use you to mark the world and the generations to come for His glory. There are blank pages left for you to fill out: (your testimony, future spouse, children, grandchildren, etc.). May you begin to experience great joy even now as you hear by faith that your children and their children to come are walking in the truth (3 John 4).

There weren't many dry eyes in the room as I finished presenting the books to them. No matter what they had done in the past, each of the women was, and is, a new creature in Christ, and God's life-changing work in their lives was cause for celebration.

God created sexual intimacy when He instituted and ordained marriage in the garden with Adam and Eve. God said that a man would leave his father and mother and that the two should become one (see Gen. 2:24). Satan has taken what God intended to be good and has distorted and perverted it. Because Satan hates God and us, he has sought to pervert and demean the gift of sex that is to be preserved for marriage.

When our spirit connects with another human being, it is the most intimate connection we can experience with another person. That is why we must marry only another believer. The physical connection through the gift of sex is the sign of the covenant of marriage. It is the outward symbol of what should take place when the husband and wife connect not only physically but also spiritually. That is how they become one.

God has created us for a relationship that is deeper, more lasting, and more fulfilling than simply a physical connection. Even as Christians who have shed the old garment of lust, we can still be vulnerable to the enemy at this point. We must guard our hearts and our minds.

Remember King David? After all of his victories, David let down his guard. In the spring, when kings typically went out to war, David stayed behind. Instead of leading his troops as he should have done, David—the giant slayer, warrior, and man after God's own heart—wandered idly up and out onto his roof. Looking out across the city, he saw a beautiful woman bathing on her rooftop. Instead of looking away, David allowed his glance to become a gaze and then a lustful stare. The thoughts that should have been taken captive were allowed to fill his mind, and David acted on his lustful thoughts.

He asked who she was. His servant told him she was Bathsheba, the wife of Uriah. David's lust and pride clouded his reasoning, and he took what belonged to another man. He had her brought to him and he had sex with her, and then he sent her back home. Thinking no one would ever know, David's hardened heart forgot the Lord. When he received word that she was pregnant, he sent for her young husband, thinking the man would go home and sleep with his wife and everyone would then think the baby belonged to him.

But David had underestimated Uriah's honor and loyalty. Uriah would not go to the comforts of his home when his fellow soldiers were out on the battlefield. Instead, he slept at the king's door along with all of David's servants. When David heard of what he had done, he called Uriah in and questioned him.

"Uriah answered David, 'The ark, Israel, and Judah are dwelling in tents, and my master Joab and his soldiers are camping in the open field. How can I enter my house to eat and drink and sleep with my wife? As surely as you live and by your life, I will not do this!'" (2 Sam. 11:11).

David told him to stay another day. He invited Uriah to eat

with him that night and got him drunk. *Surely he will go down to lie with his wife now,* David thought. But once again Uriah slept with the servants of the king.

David was desperate. The only way to cover his secret was to have Uriah die in battle. So David wrote a note to Joab, commander of the armed forces, instructing him to put Uriah in the front line of the fiercest battle and then withdraw from him so that he would die. Uriah innocently delivered his own death sentence to Joab. It happened just as David had said. After Bathsheba's time of mourning was over, David sent for her and she became his wife.

A close call, but problem solved, David must have thought. I believe the Lord gave David ample opportunity and time to confess his sin. But he was too proud or too stubborn to do so until Nathan the prophet came to see him.

Nathan told David a story of two men. One was a rich man who had a great many flocks and herds. The other was a poor man who had one little ewe lamb that he cherished. It had become like a part of his family. The rich man had guests, and he was unwilling to take from his own herd; instead he took the poor man's ewe lamb and prepared it for his guests. David was incensed and said the man who had done this should die. Nathan said, "You are the man!"

The Word of God says, "Be sure your sin will find you out" (Num. 32:23 NASB) or as another translation puts it, "Your sin will catch up with you" (HCSB). It is only confessed and repented sin that is covered by the Lord. When we try to hide our sin, God will convict us. He is patient and long-suffering, but when we refuse to confess our sin and turn from it, He will expose it because He is a holy God.

David lamented and recognized that he had sinned against the Lord, and God forgave him, but he still had to accept the consequences. The baby born to Bathsheba died. The sorrow caused by his behavior spilled over into the lives of innocent people.

Sexual immorality is a sin against God and against other humans, as David found out. It's also a sin against ourselves. First Corinthians 6:15–20 says, "Do you not know that your bodies are the members of Christ? So should I take the members of Christ and make them members of a prostitute? Absolutely not! Do you not know that anyone joined to a prostitute is one body with her? For it says, The two will become one flesh. But anyone joined to the Lord is one spirit with Him. Flee from sexual immorality! 'Every sin a person can commit is outside the body,' but the person who is sexually immoral sins against his own body. Do you not know that your body is a sanctuary of the Holy Spirit who is in you, whom you have from God? You are not your own, for you were bought at a price; therefore glorify God in your body."

As believers, we have the Spirit of Christ dwelling in us. When we join our bodies to someone who is not our spouse, we are taking the Spirit of Christ into an immoral relationship. The sin may manifest itself in our bodies. Think of sexually transmitted diseases and at least one type of cancer as dramatic examples.

If You Are a Female Uriah or a David

As it did with David, sexual sin still causes the innocent to suffer, and we see the consequences of it in our society. Perhaps you're the victim of sexual sin. You may be a female Uriah, married to a spouse who has been unfaithful. While it does appear in Scripture that unfaithfulness may be grounds for divorce,

I don't believe that divorce is the best option if the errant spouse is repentant. Instead, I would suggest that you seek counseling and that you try to reconcile with your spouse. Forgiveness is always best.

I am not saying if your spouse is abusive or habitually unfaithful that you need to stay in that situation. In the case of abuse, you may need to seek a legal separation for your safety and the safety of your children. But do not hesitate to ask for help and to seek counsel from a pastor or certified Christian counselor. Your marriage can become stronger and sweeter after the hard work of healing and restoration. That is not an empty platitude—many pastors and counselors can cite examples of couples who have put in the time and effort that reconciliation and healing require and now love each other with a deeper and purer love than they ever imagined was possible.

What if you have been a female David? God will forgive adultery. Paul makes that clear in 1 Corinthians 6:9–11, where he first lists several practices of immoral acts, including adulterers who will not inherit the kingdom of God. Then he asserts, "Such were some of you; but you were washed, but you were sanctified, but you were justified in the name of the Lord Jesus Christ and by the Spirit of our God" (NASB). Restoration will many times be painful, with long-lasting consequences. Trust the Lord and endure. He alone can bring healing and restoration to otherwise broken relationships.

If You Feel Tempted to Become a David

What if you are not in the action stage but are in the temptation stage? Take a realistic look at how immorality starts in the mind. You may begin to harbor negative and critical thoughts about your spouse, and those feelings create distance between the two of you. Then you begin to share these thoughts with a friend. Soon you are expressing them to your spouse.

As a result, you may become the nagging woman described in Proverbs: "It is better to live in the corner of a roof than in a house shared with a contentious woman" (Prov. 21:9, 25:24 NASB). "A constant dripping on a day of steady rain and a contentious woman are alike" (Prov. 27:15 NASB). Drip, drip, drip! Your husband, who was wired by God to need you to respect him, is being deprived of that respect, the one thing he needs to be the husband God has called him to be. God has commanded us as women to submit to and respect our husbands (Eph. 5).

In his book *Love and Respect,* Emerson Eggerichs says, "Wives are made to love, want love, and expect love. Many husbands fail to deliver. But as I kept studying Scripture and counseling couples, I finally saw the other half of the equation. Husbands weren't saying it much, but they were thinking, *She doesn't respect me.* Husbands are made to be respected, want respect, and expect respect. Many wives fail to deliver. The result is that five out of ten marriages land in divorce court (and that includes evangelical Christians)" (6).

So the age-old process plays itself out. As the enemy attacks you and points out the distance and lack of emotion in your marriage, you are a prime target for some other man to start moving in for the kill. And I do mean *kill!*

Someone will come across your path at work, your neighborhood, or your church—that's right, church—who recognizes all of your good qualities. That person will be complimentary, kind, and interested when you speak. You will begin to daydream about what it would be like to be married to this person instead of your spouse, who doesn't understand you. Those thoughts then evolve into wondering if you made a mistake when you married your spouse: *Maybe I missed God's will for my life. I know God never intended for me to be unhappy or unsatisfied in my marriage relationship.*

How will the Lord respond to these kinds of thoughts? He will say, "You're right! Your relationship with Me is the only one that can satisfy your deepest longings. When you allow Me to meet your need for intimacy, I will enable you to be the spouse you are supposed to be, regardless of how your spouse responds."

We must all be on guard. Second Corinthians 11:2–3 says, "For I am jealous over you with a godly jealousy, because I have promised you in marriage to one husband—to present a pure virgin to Christ. But I fear that, as the serpent deceived Eve by his cunning, your minds may be corrupted from a complete and pure devotion to Christ." We are the virgin brides of Christ. We need to live like it!

When we allow Jesus Christ to meet our deepest needs for love and significance, to fulfill our desire for More, we will be able to love our spouses and be a blessing to them. We won't be demanding that they meet our needs. We won't be draining life from them; we will instead be imparting life. There will no longer be an emotional chasm between us and our spouses. With our needs already met in a way that is beyond what any human can offer us, we will be free to practice living life from the inside out as we were meant to do.

We cannot have as our goal a good marriage, however we may define it. A good marriage takes two people. But we are responsible to God to be the wife He has called us to be. I must focus on changing my attitudes and actions, not my spouse. When I bring my thoughts under the control of Christ, God will take care of my spouse. As I begin to thank the Lord for my spouse and all of his good qualities, the way I view him and my marriage will change. Remember the Amplified Bible's translation of Ephesians 5:33? It uses a word as a synonym for respect that is a bit humorous: We will begin to *notice* our husbands!

If you have fallen prey to the lure of the enemy in either attitude or actions, confess it to the Lord and receive His forgiveness and cleansing. If you are married and need to confess unhealthy attitudes or a critical spirit toward your spouse, do that now. Remember these negative thoughts are the seedbed for later acts of unfaithfulness. A prayer like the one below will help you guard your heart and mind.

> *Dear Heavenly Father,*
>
> *I know that my mind and body belong to You. I have been purchased with the precious blood of my Savior, Jesus Christ. I confess to You that I have not kept my (mind/body) pure. I ask You to forgive me and to cleanse me from all unrighteousness. [Confess each incidence of unfaithfulness to the Lord—ask the Holy Spirit to bring them to your mind. This includes actual acts of unfaithfulness and all thoughts or fantasies.] I take back the ground I had given to the enemy, and I declare that my mind and body will be dedicated to You and used for Your glory.[1]*
>
> *In Jesus's name, Amen.*

---

1. 1 Pet. 1:18–19, 1 John 1:9, and 1 Cor. 6 are source material for this prayer.

19

Run to Win!

Do you not know that those who run in a race all run,
but only one receives the prize?
Run in such a way that you may win.
1 CORINTHIANS 9:24 (NASB)

Our oldest daughter ran her first half-marathon this past spring. She surprised us all by announcing at the beginning of the year that she had downloaded a training schedule from the Internet and was going to train to run in the Music City Marathon at the end of April. She was faithful to her goal and to her schedule. She came home from college one weekend, and we all celebrated as she put in one of her first long runs—eleven miles.

As April approached, we knew she would reach her goal. My youngest sister ran with her. My husband, our daughter's boyfriend, and I traveled to Nashville to be there with them. We stationed ourselves at the five-mile mark to cheer them on as they passed, and we hurried to the end to be there as they crossed the finish line. We yelled and cheered and took pictures. What a sense of accomplishment we felt for her as she paused to receive her medal!

This physical feat was not realized without training and discipline. It started with a decision of her will. She chose to run and knew what it would take to prepare. She was not ready to run until she had spent months preparing. The daily discipline and diligence were what enabled her to finish strong.

We began this book with an emphasis on the spirit man. That is where we start as we run the race of the Christian life. We must choose to be in right relationship with the Father through His Son, Jesus Christ. When His Spirit comes to dwell within our spirit, we have the power we need to live and run to win.

Next we focused on the soul. It is in our mind, will, and emotions that we must gain victory. We exposed wrong ways of thinking, dismantled them, and replaced them with the truth. Only after dealing with the inner man will we have any success with the outer man. It is futile to try to eradicate addictive sins of the flesh without first dealing with the wrong ways of thinking and damaged emotions that led to these addictions in the first place.

Spiritual Training and Discipline Will Equip Us to Win Life's Marathon

The Scripture at the beginning of this chapter commends us to run the race of life to win. We must not just barely make it or struggle through life at the back of the pack. We run to win! Many have compared this life to a marathon. We must train and be disciplined. There is no way we can perform well in the race of life without the discipline of training.

The apostle Paul says, "Now everyone who competes exercises self-control in everything. However, they do it to receive a perishable crown, but we an imperishable one. Therefore I do not run like one who runs aimlessly, or box like one who beats the air. Instead, I discipline my body and bring it under strict control, so that after preaching to others, I myself will not be disqualified" (1 Cor. 9:25–27).

We must live our lives focused and on purpose. We must forget what lies behind and keep our eyes on the prize of finishing well and seeing our Savior face-to-face.

The Greek word for compete is *agonia*. Do you see the English word *agony* in it? To compete sometimes feels like agony! It generally means to "contend for victory in the pubic games; it meant to fight, to wrestle, straining every nerve to the uttermost toward the goal." We must strain every fiber of our being in our quest for the prize.

That is exactly how God calls us to love Him: with all of our heart, soul, mind, and strength—with every fiber of our being. Here's the wondrous aspect of this love: Loving Him energizes and empowers us to compete.

We will receive an imperishable wreath. This wreath is not like the laurel wreaths fashioned from leafy branches that the winners of the games received in Greco-Roman and New Testament times. They were lovely and fragrant but faded quickly. Our promised victor's wreath is "not capable of corruption, an attribute of deity, that the believer receives in this life and will continue to have when this life is over"![1] Isn't that a description of eternal life as well?

That is why we discipline ourselves. We must train for the race, and we must run with perseverance. The preparation begins with surrendering our lives to Christ, and the training picks up speed as we spend time daily in prayer and in His Word.

---

1. See Spiro Zodhiates' *The Hebrew-Greek Key Study Bible,* 157, for the source of this definition.

This training of our minds and wills is as important to our finishing the race of life as physical training is to the marathon runner. That's why it is important that you cultivate the discipline of meeting with God daily. It will initially be a choice of the will that will result in a relationship that you will prize above all others. Your time with Him will become the most precious time of your day.

Meeting with God Daily Is Our Strength and Resistance Training

As you connect with the Lord daily, He will feed your spirit and strengthen and prepare you for the challenges and issues you'll be facing. As you read His words, you'll get to know Him. As you spend time with Him in prayer, He will speak to you and open your eyes and ears to begin to see as He sees. And there's an additional reason to carve out time with God, for it is in those moments that we deny ourselves and take up our cross daily to follow Him. I am not fit to hear or to follow until I have submitted my flesh and sat at His feet.

Remember the diagram from the first pages of this book? Here it is again:

This diagram portrays our restored relationship with God through the cross. The spirit man, now in control, enables us to live from the inside out. The body is relegated to a place of lesser importance. But notice this:

Saved for More

It's not absent from the diagram. Rather, it is under control. Once we are filled with and led by the Spirit, we will be able to see life from an eternal vantage point—with "Spirit" eyes.

In their book *The Sacred Romance: Drawing Closer to the Heart of God,* John Eldredge and Brent Curtis make an insightful statement about the ability to see with Spirit eyes: "Entering into the sacred romance begins with eyes to see and ears to hear. Where would we be today if Eve had looked at the serpent with different eyes? If she had seen at once that the beautiful creature with the charming voice and the reasonable proposition was in fact a fallen angel bent on the annihilation of the human race. If only her ear had been in tune with the voice of her Father. If only her eyes had seen as He sees" (145).

Because we are no longer citizens of this world and are living in hostile territory, it is imperative that we learn to see and hear in our spirit man. Many Christians believe in the importance of a quiet time. If you are like many others, you have started one more than once, but have never been successful at maintaining it. Are you ready to try again?

20

It's about Time

You will seek Me and find Me
when you search for Me with all your heart.
JEREMIAH 29:13

*T*he Nielsen Company, which compiles statistics on TV watching, has determined that the average American spends more than four hours each day watching television. Add to that the fact that Americans of all ages are spending more and more time connected to the Web using cell phones, PDAs, Blackberrys, and iPods, and it's no wonder that finding time to connect with the Creator of the universe seems impossible. Once you start, though, you'll find that you cannot let a day go by without your time with Him.

Commit to a Time and Select a Place

It is essential that you have a time and a place for your appointment with the Lord. It can be a location as simple as the end of a sofa or a chair in your bedroom. Mine is a chair. Beside it is a decorative box that contains everything I need. I call it a "treasure box," though some of my friends have referred to it as a "toolbox." It definitely contains both treasure and tools.

My box contains:

- a one-year chronological Bible
- devotional books
- a hymnal
- a prayer notebook
- a journal
- pens and note cards
- 3" x 5" cards
- tissues

I begin my time with a brief prayer, asking God to speak to me. I surrender my will and ask for His alone. Then I read that day's portion of Scripture from the One Year Bible. Each day contains a portion from the Old Testament, New Testament, Psalms, and Proverbs. I have been doing this for years. It is the easiest way I have found to read the Bible through in a year.

You may ask why it is important to read the entire Bible. You will be amazed as you see that our God truly is the same yesterday, today, and forever. God has revealed Himself to humans from the beginning of time. He prepared the way for His Son to come to earth, and the Son is the exact representation of the Father. You read the Bible to get to know the author.

Second Timothy 3:16–17 (NLT) says, "All Scripture is inspired by God and is useful to teach us what is true and to make us realize what is wrong in our lives. It corrects us when we are wrong and teaches us to do what is right. God uses it to prepare and equip his people to do every good work." Do we need another reason?

After prayer and Scripture reading, I read from a devotional book. I have used many through the years. My favorites are Oswald Chambers' *My Utmost for His Highest,* Amy Carmichael's *Whispers of His Power* and *Edges of His Ways,* Mrs. Charles E. Cowman's *Streams in the Desert,* and my husband Steve Gaines's *Morning Manna.* (They're in the bibliography, in case you'd like a copy.)

Effective Prayers Avail Much

It is now time to enter into prayer. For my prayer requests I use a loose-leaf notebook that has dividers and tabs to separate the sections. To help you get started, following is a list of my sections in the order in which I've arranged them:

1. *Praise.* It contains pages of mostly Scripture that I pray back to the Father in worship and adoration.
2. *My family.* I use plastic sheet protectors to insert pictures. I enjoy looking at my family while I pray for them. Many times I lay my hands on each picture as I pray. There are separate sheets for each family member with Scriptures on them that I pray for them, as well as specific requests. When God answers a prayer, I record the answer and date it. Recording answers is a great boost to your faith.
3. *My church.* In this section is a list of all the ministers and staff that work at our church. I pray through this list once or twice a week.

4. *Friends.* Among our friends are many who are in front-line positions for the cause of Christ. I want to be faithful to pray for them and their families.

5. *Intercession.* When people ask you to pray for them, often it is best to pray with them at the moment they make the request. Then write down their names and requests, and when you get home, transfer it to the intercession section of your prayer notebook. You won't be able to pray daily for all of these requests, but you can work through them at least once a week.

6. *Government officials.* This section contains names of national leaders, such as our president and his cabinet and the Supreme Court. It also contains names of our state leaders, such as our governor and senators and representatives. The third list is the names of our city's mayor and council.

7. *The world.* This section contains an atlas. The Spirit sometimes directs me to pray for a certain country. Many times I will pray for missionaries or people from our church who are on a mission trip in a certain part of the world. I always enjoy looking at the country and many times finding the very city where they will be working and praying over it.

There will be some sections, such as the one for your family, that you will pray for daily. You may find yourself praying for a few requests every day from the other sections, working through the entire list each week. Allow the Spirit to direct you. As you are praying, you may think of someone the Lord is prompting you to call or to send a written note. Take one of your three-by-five-inch cards and jot the name and action down. This helps keep you from being distracted and is also a separate record that will keep you from forgetting what the Lord has told you to do. After your prayer time, you can do what the Lord has prompted.

It is always good to close your time with the Lord in worship. You may want to pray a psalm back to Him. You can sing praise songs to Him. You can use your hymnal or a CD of recorded music. Don't be afraid to use your voice in praise. God gave it to you, and He knows what it sounds like! I would never be asked to sing a solo in church, but I have performed many of them for the Lord.

When You Fast

The early Christians engaged in a practice that many of us are unfamiliar with. They fasted. They took for granted that fasting was a part of the spiritual discipline of any believer. Acts 13:2–3 describes the Antioch church: "As they were ministering to the Lord and fasting, the Holy Spirit said, 'Set apart for Me Barnabas and Saul for the work that I have called them to.' Then after they had fasted, prayed, and laid hands on them, they sent them off."

Fasting is linked with prayer many times in the Bible. It is also obvious that Jesus expected His followers to fast. He said, "When you fast (Matt. 6:16 NIV)," not "If." He also said that we should fast not to be seen by others, but by our Father. "Your Father who sees in secret will reward you," Jesus explained (Matt. 6:18b).

One of the best books on fasting I have found was written by Bill Bright. *Seven Basic Steps to Successful Fasting and Prayer* is a concise discussion of the various types of fasts. (You'll find publishing information in the bibliography.)

Pray when prompted by the Lord to fast and He will direct you. You might begin by skipping one meal. It is ideal to spend that time with the Lord. Instead of partaking of physical food, partake of spiritual food. The Lord may then expand your fast to a full day or three days. When I have fasted in the past, I have viewed each hunger pang as a call to prayer. I can't explain fasting any more than I can explain prayer—but I know it works!

Fasting is a powerful tool in demolishing counterfeit strongholds. If you continue to struggle with knocking one down, the Lord may be saying to you, "Make My will your food." When you deprive your body of physical nourishment and instead partake of spiritual food, your sense of God's presence and desire for Him heightens.

The Bible records many accounts of people who fasted:

- The great prophets of God fasted. Moses and Elijah both fasted. (See Deut. 9:7–20 and 1 Kings 19:1–9.)
- Queen Esther and her household fasted, as did the people in her family's city, at a time when their lives were threatened (Esther 4:15–16). God answered their fast by sparing their lives and destroying their enemies.
- Jesus fasted. When He did, He told His disciples, "I have food to eat that you don't know about" (John 4:32). He was partaking of spiritual food, and the Father was nourishing Him in His inner man.
- The early Christians fasted.

These examples illustrate how God honors fasting and how it sharpens the senses so that the promptings of the Holy Spirit are discerned.

Meditate on God's Word

Another practice that will strengthen your inner person and restore your soul is meditating on the Word of God. Psalm 19:7–11 beautifully describes the riches of the Word of God: "The law of the LORD is perfect, restoring the soul; the testimony of the LORD is sure, making wise the simple. The precepts of the LORD are right, rejoicing the heart; the commandments of the LORD are pure, enlightening the eyes. The fear of the LORD is clean, enduring forever; the judgments of the LORD are true; they are righteous all together. They are more desirable than gold, yes, than much fine gold; sweeter also than honey and the drippings of the honeycomb. Moreover, by them Your servant is warned; in keeping them there is great reward."

Meditating on God's Word should be a natural outgrowth of reading the words He has given us. It's an active and dynamic process that will change the way we think, and the way we think will eventually change the way we act.

You can meditate on God's Word by taking it with you. Try writing specific passages on three-by-five-inch cards, and keep them with you during the day. You can also meditate on the Word by playing Scripture choruses or even listening to the Bible on CD. In our home, the only music allowed in the mornings is praise music. I want our children to leave the house with the praises of our Lord in their minds and on their lips.

Memorize God's Word

This past year has been a very difficult one in many ways. Have you ever experienced a period of time when you felt it was all you could do to keep your head above water? Then you understand what I'm talking about. A friend gave me a ring-bound stack of three-by-five-inch cards with a plastic cover. I began to write down Scriptures the Lord was using to speak to me and the promises He was using in my life. I took that little pack of cards everywhere I went. I was constantly reviewing the Scriptures, and before I knew it, I had most of them memorized. God's Word sustained me and allowed me to break free of the circumstances that were seeking to weigh me down.

My husband has systematically memorized Scripture since our early years of dating. He started with the Navigators Topical Memory System (see www.navigators.org for more information). I call him "my walking concordance." Anytime I need to know the location of a verse, I just ask him.

It starts with that one step: setting aside time. Ask God to help you in this first step. He promises you'll find Him when you take time to seek Him.

21

Follow Me As I Follow Christ

Be imitators of me, just as I also am of Christ.
1 CORINTHIANS 11:1 (NASB)

Do you know the expression "Her life is an open book"? It is particularly true when observing Christians who model a life of More. Learning from someone who has traveled further in her walk with Christ than you have will challenge you to grow spiritually. I have always sought out older women who had a vibrant relationship with Jesus and learned from them.

Another way I have been discipled is through the writings of other Christians. Many of my favorite disciplers are dead! I so look forward to meeting them in heaven. Meanwhile, they live on through their writings, and their influence for Christ continues.

I encourage you to invest in Christian books. There is an often-quoted proverb that states: "Readers are leaders and leaders are readers." As a former teacher and a forever book-lover,

I underline passages and dog-ear pages that I want to find later. Many of my books are beloved, and I can see certain passages in my mind and know exactly where to open to find them. Don't be afraid to mark up your books! When you do so, they become a part of you.

Paul said to the Corinthians, "You yourselves are our letter, written on our hearts, recognized and read by everyone, since it is plain that you are Christ's letter, produced by us, not written with ink but with the Spirit of the living God; not on stone tablets but on tablets that are hearts of flesh" (2 Cor. 3:2–3). Stories of love and devotion to Christ that are being written out in lives that are consecrated to the Lord are effective motivators and inspiration for us as well.

In his book *Growing True Disciples: New Strategies for Producing Genuine Followers of Christ,* George Barna states emphatically the importance of being a passionate follower of Christ: "To determine whether you are a disciple, the relevant question concerns your level of commitment: *To what are you absolutely, fanatically devoted?* Jesus did not minister, die, and rise from the dead merely to enlist fans. He gave everything He had to create a community of uncompromising zealots—raving, unequivocal, undeterable, no-holds-barred spiritual revolutionaries. He has no room for lukewarm followers" (98–99).

Passion for Christ is caught more than it is taught. If we want our children, those we are mentoring and influencing, to love Jesus Christ, we must love Him with all of our heart, soul, mind, and strength. The life and joy brought about by this lack of compromise and total devotion will draw them to Jesus.

A close friend of mine, Joni Shankles, wrote a tribute to one of her mentors. With her permission, I have included it with the prayer that we will all be living, breathing letters of the grace of Christ for all to read:

I love everything about books. From the sound a new hardback makes when you open it for the first time to the familiar comfort of an often read favorite, I love it all. I am drawn to bookstores and bookshelves everywhere to look, to dream, to learn.

Over the last several years as my hunger to please God has grown, I have turned often to the writings of great men and women of God for insight and direction on how to live a vital, obedient Christian life. I have spent hundreds of dollars buying books recommended by friends and Bible teachers. I have spent countless hours poring over the lives and teachings of godly men and women, mining each for gems of wisdom on how to apply Scripture to real life situations. My bookshelves hold books on such topics as parenting, marriage, Christian growth, prayer, spiritual warfare, and friendship. Yet it may surprise you to know that the best book I've ever read on any of these topics is not on a shelf in my office. As a matter of fact, the best book I've ever read cannot be found in any booksellers' catalog or ordered online. The best book I've ever read about passionately and obediently following Christ isn't a book at all . . . it's a person, my friend.

In the pages of her life I have seen God's Word come literally to life—in her home, in her ministry, in her responses to strangers and difficult people, and even in her van as she goes about the daily routine of life.

In every arena God allows her to enter, she brings the fragrance of the Lord Jesus, touching lives with the grace, love, and hope that can only be found in Him.

I have watched my friend "study her man"—learning what her husband likes, what makes him smile, those special things that communicate "I love you!" I have listened to her speak to him and about him in love, always focusing on what he is doing right and not dwelling on any wrong. I have seen her love for him spill out of her eyes and down her cheeks as she lifted up prayers for God to heal him and care for him during a difficult surgery. And because of her example, I am a better wife.

I have listened to her tell stories of God proving His faithfulness to her children and heard her excitement when she tells of some new spiritual truth one of them is learning. I have watched as she prepares a special snack for them before she picks them up from school, and in that and in so many other small ways she communicates to them "You are special!" I have seen in her children the fruit of loving discipline and fervent prayer. And because of her, I am a better mother.

I love to hear my friend talk about Jesus and to see the fire of excitement in her eyes as she speaks of His love and faithfulness. I have seen in her life a demonstration of the peace and safety that comes from living under His authority. I have heard testimonies of the often painful but always loving way God is molding her into Christ's image. Knowing that her failures have been places to begin again have brought comfort, seeing her triumphs has fanned hope into flame. And I am a better Christian.

I have seen my friend leave an extra large tip for waitresses and waiters, doormen and valets, and have heard her give each a word of encouragement, leaving them with the lingering aroma of Christ. I have listened to her apologize to unbelievers for the rude conduct of others who bear the name of Christ. I marvel still at how she is constantly aware that no matter where she goes, everyone is looking for hope, for Jesus, and how she wants them to find Him in her actions. And I am a better witness.

For as long as I've known her, I have watched my friend set aside blocks of time each week for in-depth Bible study. As I hear my friend teach from God's Word, I know she is teaching what she knows. Her every conversation bears the evidence that she is learning something from the Lord daily. And I read my Bible more, looking for the God she knows.

And what I know about prayer, about really communicating with God, about interceding on someone else's behalf—I have learned from my friend as she blesses the Lord and uses His very Word, verses of Scripture, to form petitions for herself, her family, or a lost family member. And I want to be on my knees more.

Yes, my friend is the best book about living a godly life that I have ever read. But you see, when I listen and watch and read her life, the result is not a desire to be like her. When I read her life, I am filled with a longing to know better the Jesus that lives so beautifully through her.

There have been those who have told me through the years, "You are going to be a writer. You will write a book someday." But the only book I desire to leave on this earth is one like my friend is writing—the story of a godly life filled with pages of obedience and God's grace, a story written in love for my husband and children to read. And may their response be, "I want to know Jesus more."

For our lives to be living letters, we must be disciplined as we run the race the Lord has set before us. I have some advice: Don't run alone! Ask the Lord for a mentor (someone further along in her walk with Christ) and for godly friends. The accountability and encouragement from godly friends are sometimes just what we need to get our second wind and push us toward the finish line. Remember, we are running to win!

22

Cheering Us On!

Therefore since we also have such
a large cloud of witnesses surrounding us, let us lay aside
every weight and the sin that so easily ensnares us,
and run with endurance the race that lies before us.

HEBREWS 12:1

*E*ach of our four children is or was involved in extracurricular activities. I have sat through too many baseball, basketball, and football games to count. Our son played sports, and all three of our girls were cheerleaders in junior high and high school. I know what it's like to be in the stands, praying and cheering for your children—desiring for them to do their best because you love them and you want them to be pleased with their performance. Win or lose, I was always so proud of them, simply because they were mine!

One football game of my son's stands out in my memory. The game was tied at the end of the fourth quarter. We went into overtime. We tied again. We went into another overtime. You guessed it; both teams scored. We finally won the game in the fifth overtime! Fans in the stands were on their feet, yelling and cheering for their team. I felt as if I had been out on that field!

In *The Back Door to Your Teen's Heart,* Melissa Trevathan and Sissy Goff tell a story originally told by Bob Benson as he recounted his own experience as a parent in the stands. He asked his son, a drummer in a high school marching band, to describe what it felt like to be out on the field:

> I asked Patrick if he could describe what it was like marching toward the stands filled with cheering parents and friends, playing wide open with all that paint on his face and finally coming to attention as the last echoes of the music of the concluding song of the final show are lost in the noise of the crowd. He grinned as if it were impossible to explain. I told him that if he thought it was exciting on the field, he should just wait until a day somewhere, sometime when he was a dad at a state championship. And then he would see his kid turn and march toward him in perfect step with a hundred other kids, his head high and his back straight, beating fifty pounds of drums as if it were his task to set the tempo for the whole world. I told him if I was still around, I wanted to be sitting there with him. And then we can talk about what thrilling really is.

My thinking about this nudged me into some further thoughts about the heavenly Father. This one who is calling us. We all tend to believe (or at least fear) that the God who calls us is watching us. It makes all the difference in the world where we think he is sitting! As long as we think of him as the judge in the pressbox who is checking for smudges on our white shoes, for the misplayed notes, for marching out of step, for our hats falling off, or any one of a dozen other things that can happen to us in a performance, it is hard to keep from living our whole lives in fear of a button coming off our tunics.

It was Jesus himself who reminded us that we were to call him Father—"Abba Father"—which is a lot more like calling him "Dad." I think Jesus was telling us that our Father is the one in the stands who is standing on the seat, waving his coat in a circle over his head, with tears of pride and happiness running down his face. (114–115)

Step out on the field and hear your Father as He calls your name. He loves you, and He is rooting for you! Look up! The stands are full of those who have gone before, and they are cheering for you too. He has given you everything you need to succeed and to be carried off the field when you breathe your last breath, escorted by the angels of heaven as they bring you into His presence.

My heart's desire is that you might know the joy I feel as I anticipate that glorious day! I am applauding and cheering for you too! Let's cross that line with our heads held high, ears tuned to the applause of our Father.

Yes, dear friend, there is More! More for now and for all of eternity. Don't waste another minute. Kneel at the foot of the cross. Surrender to the One who knows you best and loves you most! The More you have been searching for is yours in the name of Jesus Christ.